WHEN YOU COME TO A FORK
IN THE ROAD, TAKE IT!

Also by Yogi Berra:

THE YOGI BOOK:
"I REALLY DIDN'T SAY EVERYTHING I SAID"

YOGI BERRA'S BASEBALL BOOK:
THE GAME AND HOW TO PLAY IT

YOGI:
IT AIN'T OVER

WHEN YOU COME TO A FORK IN THE ROAD, TAKE IT!

*Inspiration and Wisdom from
One of Baseball's Greatest Heroes*

YOGI BERRA

with DAVE KAPLAN

HYPERION

NEW YORK

The authors would like to acknowledge the valuable assistance of editor Leslie Wells in making this book, as well as Ed Berlin, Michael Harriot, and David Vigliano of Vigliano & Associates.

ISBN 0-7868-6775-2

Book design by Casey Hampton

FIRST EDITION

10 9 8 7 6 5 4 3 2

For my favorite nine—Lindsay, Larry, Gretchen, Bridgette,
Whitney, Christopher, Andrew, Nicholas, and Maria.
I will always be thankful for the presence of wise and
wonderful grandchildren, whom I each love so much.

—YOGI BERRA

To Naomi and Leah, Emily and Eva—
my daily inspiration.

—DAVE KAPLAN

CONTENTS

WHEN YOU COME TO A FORK IN THE ROAD, TAKE IT!

WHEN YOU COME TO A FORK
IN THE ROAD, TAKE IT

A proud tradition of Yankee catchers: *(left to right)* Bill Dickey, me, Elston Howard, and Thurman Munson.
Berra Archives

Throughout life you come to serious forks in the road—decisions. Which path do you choose? Sometimes it's tough. People are always afraid of making the wrong choice. But no matter what decision you make—taking a job, getting married, buying a house, whatever it is—you shouldn't look back. Trust your instincts.

The beauty of baseball is that you always have forks in the road—decisions that could mean the difference between winning and losing. If you're a manager, when do you take a pitcher out if he's tiring? Do you hit and run with slow runners on base? Like they say, decisions, decisions. Joe Torre does a great job as the Yankee manager; it always seems he makes the right decision. He trusts his instincts.

But he also trusts his bench coach, Don Zimmer, to bounce ideas off of. Zim has a lot of experience. He's Joe's security blanket. Between them, the Yankees are always on the right road.

. . .

I've always done things that *feel* right. I've also been lucky. Throughout my life, I've always had my family behind me, helping me make the right choices. My first big life decision was at age fourteen, when I wanted to quit school after eighth grade to go to work. My parents, the principal, and the parish priest all had a conference and tried to talk me into continuing, but I was a lousy student and pretty stubborn and felt I was wasting my time. I remember a teacher once asking me, "Don't you know anything?" and I said I don't even suspect anything.

They finally all agreed I'd be just as well off working and handing over what I made to Mom. I realize now this was a major turning point in my life, and I was fortunate. Education is a necessary part of a young person's life. Very few who quit school early on ever wind up successful when they get older.

But the decision was for my own good, and it wouldn't have been made without Mom and Pop's approval. Also, without my parents—and my three older brothers—I wouldn't have been allowed to pursue my dream of playing baseball. Things worked out well, because if not for baseball, I might still be in the shoe factory. So I didn't have regrets about taking that fork in the road to leave school. Except, looking back now, I do feel a little remiss about not finishing. It's a void in my life, and it's why Carm and I arranged trust funds for our three sons, Larry, Tim, and Dale, to guarantee them a college education. Because of my situation, I was very anxious they get as much schooling as they could.

One of my biggest decisions ever was over fifty years ago, asking a beautiful waitress at Biggie's restaurant in St. Louis out on a date—then eventually asking her to marry me. I didn't have much confidence back then. I was bashful, nervous, and not good-looking. I could hardly believe my luck that Carmen liked me as much as I liked her. I soon knew as sure as anything that I wanted to spend the rest of my life with her.

After marrying Carm in 1949, we came to a few forks in the road—tough life decisions. At the time, I was making only $12,000 a year with the Yankees. After the season, we lived in St. Louis where I grew up (although Carm grew up in Salem, Missouri) and where we had real tight-knit families. Everything and everybody we knew were there. I even worked at nearby Ruggeri's restaurant as a head waiter in the off-season.

But we were kind of torn. There were more opportunities in the East. My baseball career was there. We wanted to start a family. Believe me, it was tough leaving everything behind when we finally decided to move to the New York area in 1951. But it was the right thing for us, because we made a good new life, and got more comfortable financially. I doubt the same could've happened back home.

Carm and I talk over everything. The decision to leave St. Louis was ours. The big decision to become a coach with Casey Stengel and the Mets, and not stay with the Yankees in another job after being let go as manager in 1964,

4

was ours. As it turned out, things were good coaching with the Mets. It was the right move, secure and safe. That's why Carm didn't want me to become their manager when Gil Hodges died in 1972. But I was at a crossroads—another fork in the road. I was forty-six years old and wanted to manage again, to prove I could. I didn't think I'd ever get another chance. Carm and my old pal Joe Garagiola thought I was foolish, and tried to talk me out of it. They thought I had a great job, since coaches last forever and managers don't. But I had a strong desire to take the Mets job, and did. I relished the challenge and never looked back. A year later, we won the National League pennant.

I think that's what all these graduation speakers mean when they quote me, "When you see the fork in the road, take it." Make a firm decision. Make sure it feels right. Learn from the choice you make. Don't second-guess yourself—there's no need to give yourself ulcers. But my advice on big life decisions is to get advice if you can. Talk it over with a parent, a mentor, a teacher, or a coach. They've had more life experience. They've got more miles on them, they can help you get on the right path. When I see my grandchildren choosing colleges and graduating from them and looking for the right job, I'm very proud. I see them making informed choices. They're coming to the fork in the road, and they know what to do.

2

IT'S NEVER HAPPENED IN WORLD SERIES HISTORY, AND IT HASN'T HAPPENED SINCE

The perfect ending to a perfect game—
October 8, 1956. *AP Photos*

When people ask what my biggest thrill was, I always say catching Don Larsen's perfect game in the 1956 World Series was right up there. That's because it happened in the high drama of a World Series. And against such a powerful team, the Brooklyn Dodgers.

As the catcher I was pretty calm—I was so concentrated on calling a good game—but I was pretty nervous going into that last inning. And Don's palms were sweaty, too. The game was still close, we were only winning 2–0, and I didn't want him to worry about the perfect game. Nobody said anything to Larsen all game for fear of jinxing him. But before the ninth inning, I told him, "Let's get the first guy. That's the main thing." And Gooney Bird—that's what we called him—did just that and even better. He made history and all hell broke loose.

I learned a lot about handling pressure by playing in all those World Series. Basically, I learned to relax. In a World

Series, emotion is intense and people are intense. Everything's intense. But you can't think about it or let your mind wander. You have to concentrate on your job and have fun doing it. For some reason, I blocked out all the hysteria about a Subway Series, which we had so many times against Brooklyn. On radio and TV and in all the newspapers, that's all you heard, saw, and read. New York City went crazy when the Yankees played the Dodgers. What we did mattered to millions of people—the World Series was an earthshaking event back then. To me, it was fun; it was just baseball. The biggest lesson I learned about World Series pressure was simple: You can't be afraid of making a mistake. There's always the next inning, or the next day. Life goes on.

Every ballplayer has a hunger to play in—and win—the World Series. I consider myself real lucky playing in—and winning—more World Series than anyone. The rewards were great in terms of pride and our pockets. Way before the big money came into baseball, we'd almost double our salaries with a World Series winning share. And we took this very seriously. Hank Bauer used to warn any new players on the Yankees, "Don't mess with my money," meaning you'd better do your job so we get into the World Series again.

Like any pressure-packed situation, a World Series can bring out the best and worst in people. It sure as heck did with me. If you play in front of 65,000 people or go on a job interview or take a driver's test, you're going to be nervous. It's human nature. Ballplayers who never took a pill had to take sleeping pills during the World Series.

Pressure means nervousness. You're terrified to make a

goof. Everyone's eyes, it seems, are focused on you. How well you perform in a pressure situation is determined by your own approach. You have to think positively. You have to have confidence. You can't fear making a mistake that will hurt your team.

That's easy for me to say now, because my first World Series in 1947—my rookie year—was one of the more forgettable experiences of my life. It was great because we won it, and I hit the first pinch home run in World Series history. But the idea of losing the Series because of one of my mistakes—and costing my teammates the winner's share—made me a nervous wreck. I don't believe I ever looked worse behind the plate.

Game 4 was the one I'll never forget. Bill Bevens was one out away from pitching the first no-hitter in World Series history. We had a 2–1 lead in the ninth, with two outs, runner on first for the Dodgers. When the runner, Al Gionfriddo, went to steal second, I made a high throw and he was safe. Then we walked the next guy and Cookie Lavagetto followed by smacking one against the wall—the Dodgers' only hit—and both runs scored. It was a devastating loss, especially for Bevens, yet nobody felt worse than me. If I had made a better throw on Gionfriddo's steal, Bevens would have gotten the no-hitter and we would have won. In fact, the Dodgers ran ragged on me that Series, stealing everything except my glove. I was so bad that even Connie Mack, the Philadelphia A's owner who was a real gentleman, told the papers, "Never in a World Series have I seen such awful catching."

Still, we won, and the check for $5,830 for a week's worth—our World Series share—helped soothe things. The check was even bigger than my whole year's salary, which was $5,000.

I chalked that Series up to an expensive lesson. Ignore the criticism. Learn from your mistakes. Keep believing in yourself. A lot of people said I was humiliated and shell-shocked, and that I'd be through as a major-league player. Truth is, I was disappointed in my play, not crushed. And by 1949, the first of our five straight World Series championships, I had gained much more confidence. Bill Dickey had helped make me a better catcher. I proved I was no clown behind the plate. I was less nervous. I learned to block out the crowd noise and matured as a player. The pressure of the World Series didn't scare me anymore, and I got better and better. In the '53 Series against the Dodgers I hit .417. In '56, I caught Larsen's perfect game and hit .360 that Series, including two homers in Game 7. Only two days before, my mom, who had diabetes and was undergoing an operation to remove a leg, told me on the phone to hit a home run for her. When I hit my first homer in that Game 7, I was running around the bases and thinking to myself, "That's for you, Mom." It was a day late, but I got another one for her in the same game.

Like anything, a little success does wonders for your confidence. Whitey Ford was the greatest World Series pitcher I ever saw, because he was so calm and cool and such a positive thinker. They said he had ice water in his veins because nothing ever fazed him. He had confidence and cockiness.

He was flip and funny off the field, but on it he was deadly serious and self-assured.

Nobody can help but be nervous in the World Series—or at a job interview, or giving a presentation, or when you're called on in class—but you have to channel that nervousness. Enjoy the moment—it's a great experience. I was real excited and proud to be in the World Series. I got a kick out of seeing all the police, the celebrities, the politicians, the reporters, and the baseball people. Got a kick out of the electricity and frenzy of the fans and the city. I loved the charged atmosphere and the adrenaline rush. I considered myself lucky to be part of it all. Except for my first World Series, I had the utmost confidence in myself. I was no longer a basket of nerves. I loved the challenge and the competition. I never doubted myself again and never got jumpy on the field again, except on the afternoon of October 8, 1956. That's when I took a flying leap into Don Larsen's arms.

NOBODY DID NOTHIN'
TO NOBODY

In the middle of our dynasty: Mickey Mantle, Casey
Stengel, me, and Hank Bauer. *Berra Archives*

When you're part of a team, you stand up for your teammates. Your loyalty is to them. You protect them through good and bad, because they'd do the same for you. The Yankee teams I played on were real close-knit guys always pulling for each other, always looking out for one another—on the field and off. Everybody got along, everybody fit in.

When Elston Howard joined us in 1955, he was the first black man on the Yankees, but we always made sure Ellie felt part of us. There was segregation in the South, and Ellie was forced to stay in separate hotels in Florida in those days. George Weiss, our general manager, got some heat for taking so long to get a black player, but we players always made Ellie feel like he belonged. We always tried to make things as pleasant for him as we could. Phil Rizzuto was like a father to him, always talking to him. I used to go with Ellie shopping for clothes and to the movies, and he always played in our card games. If a bunch of us went out, we asked Ellie to come along.

As I said, we were a team. We ate together. We socialized and played cards together. Sometimes we went out with our wives together. Unfortunately, that's what happened on May 16, 1957, when we took Billy Martin out to celebrate his birthday—his twenty-ninth. Billy was a bachelor, but Whitey Ford, Mickey Mantle, Hank Bauer, and I brought our wives, since we didn't have a game the next afternoon. I also brought Johnny Kucks, who was one of our young pitchers, to join us. Carmen thought going out would help relax me since I wasn't hitting too well at the time. She suggested we all see the singer Johnny Ray at the Waldorf and then go to the Copacabana, which was a real popular club on West 51st Street, to see Sammy Davis.

Well, a drunk customer began heckling Sammy Davis, and Bauer told the guy to shut up. Then one of the guy's friends challenged Hank to a fight. We all got up but were separated from the drunk's friends by the restaurant staff. The drunk went into the men's room, and minutes later when Hank went in, the drunk was knocked out on the floor with a broken nose. It looked like Hank had slugged him, but in actuality it was one of the Copacabana bouncers. We all left through the kitchen, hoping nobody would see us or we'd be in big trouble. But Hank got a call from a crime reporter at 4:30 in the morning because the drunk was at the police station swearing out a warrant for his arrest. The next day all hell broke loose. "Bauer in Brawl in Copa" was the headline on page one, and George Weiss was furious. He was sure Billy Martin had started the whole thing and called all of us into his office to get the real story, but nobody admitted hitting the guy. Then he called me aside, I think knowing I was always honest and would tell what really happened. That's when I said, "Nobody did nothin' to nobody." Still, Weiss was convinced we were all covering up to protect Martin, and he was real angry we'd gone out on the town. The owner, Dan Topping, thought we had hurt the Yankee image and immediately fined us all $1,000, which was a lot of money in those days.

But in a way, the Copacabana incident brought us even closer together. We all were angry about the fines, which came before the hearing and made it look like we were all guilty. And Weiss was still angry at us for being at the Copa. I think he thought we had no business going out with our wives, and that made us angry, too. We were in third place when the Copacabana thing happened. I won't say it rallied us, but we did go on to win the pennant. As it turned out, the case was dropped for lack of evidence, but Billy still got the blame—he was traded to Kansas City soon after.

Almost twenty years later, Billy got in more trouble with the Yankees when he was managing and I was one of his coaches. The Yankees in 1977 were much different from the Yankees I played on—there was bickering and some big egos. Some of the players barely spoke to each other. One day in Boston, on national television, Billy pulled Reggie Jackson out of the game because he didn't think he hustled on a ball. Reggie was a dandy. He was quite high on himself as a star. He'd ask me and Ellie Howard, who was also coaching, where he would fit on the great Yankee teams we played on. We'd say, "fifth outfielder." We just wanted to bring his ego down.

Billy had had enough of Reggie that day and was screaming at him in the dugout about not hustling. Reggie yelled something back, and Billy charged at him—I feared he was going to take a swing at him. I immediately bear-hugged Billy—Ellie grabbed him, too—and forced him away. It was an ugly incident, something you never want to see guys on the same team doing, let alone with 30 million people watching. We had to protect Billy from himself. He was a great manager but terribly explosive. I don't want to think about what would've happened if he'd hit Reggie in front of everybody—he was half his size and half his age. It wouldn't have been good. Thankfully, in the end nobody did nothin' to nobody.

"SLUMP? I AIN'T IN NO SLUMP . . . I JUST AIN'T HITTING"

Playing for the Stockham Post in American Legion ball was an education. I learned a lot about baseball, picked up the nickname "Yogi," and got a chance to travel.
Berra Archives

Everybody has slumps. Hitters and pitchers struggle for no reason. Your good moods suddenly become bad moods. Who knows why? As Catfish Hunter used to say, "The sun don't shine on the same dog's ass all the time." When I went through spells when I wasn't getting any hits, people said I was tired. But I was always a little tired—even when I was on a hitting streak—so that wasn't it. I've simply decided that to break a slump, all you can do is keep the faith and keep working hard and hope that your luck changes.

I've seen guys do different things to snap out of slumps. They experiment. They change their stance. They grip the bat tighter. They think too much. They take bad advice. They often make things even worse. When I had an off year in 1957, I wasn't overly worried. I had dropped to .251 but struck out only twenty-four times and still hit my regular number of homers. The rest of the time I hit the ball, nothing dropped in. It was one of those years. Still, I got tips in the mail from people—plumbers, dentists, you name it—about what I was doing wrong. They meant well. And even my own boss, George Weiss, thought something was wrong so he wanted me to try glasses—he thought I had "tired eyes." I wore them for about a week. They didn't help.

After the season, the Yankees had me go to the Mayo Clinic for some tests. But everything was fine. The doctor said I had great eyesight and the best reflexes of anyone he ever saw. Bottom line is slumps happen. They're hard to explain. The big thing is not to change who you are. Think positive. Don't press. Change a few things, but only to get comfortable. I never changed my stance. I tried a lighter bat. I'm a funny guy. If I'm not hitting, I don't blame me. I blame the bat. I try a new one.

If nothing works during a slump, my advice is to try something new. Talk to others you trust. If all else fails, change your routine. When I was managing the Mets in 1973, my coaches and I were at a loss when Tug McGraw, our best relief pitcher, was blowing leads. We tried everything to get him straightened out. Analyzed his delivery. Sent him to the minors. Nothing was helping. Then I surprised everyone—Tug included—by giving him a couple starts, hoping that'd snap him out of his funk. Actually, that sort of helped do the trick. Tug got hit pretty good as a starter, but when he returned to the bullpen, he was the old Tug McGraw. He found his rhythm again. In his last twenty appearances, he did not blow a lead. Whatever the reason, his slump was over and he became our inspiration, shouting,

"You gotta believe" all the time as we went on to win the pennant.

Some slumps are mechanical. Some are psychological. To get out of them you need concentration and luck. Like I said, you can't think and hit at the same time. No rapid reflex action can happen consciously. I think there's too much thinking and theorizing about hitting, and not enough humdrum repetition. I believe you develop good habits through practice. And I believe bad habits can slip in through different things—injury, carelessness, fatigue, worry, whatever. More than anything, you have to have a good frame of mind to break a slump. As you see, I didn't even like to call a slump a slump. I just temporarily wasn't hitting.

WE HAVE A GOOD TIME TOGETHER, EVEN WHEN WE'RE NOT TOGETHER

Marrying Carm on January 26, 1949, I felt like king of The Hill. *Berra Archives*

What can I say about Carmen, except that she's still beautiful and intelligent and has put up with a lot being married to me for over fifty years. It isn't easy being a ballplayer's wife, especially when you're in charge of three young boys at home. But Carm's been my partner the whole time, and believe me, her sacrifices and support were truly vital to my baseball career.

The main thing is we've always been dedicated to each other while keeping a sense of humor about everything. When I was playing ball, she raised our three sons by herself—did all the dirty-neck inspections, helped with schoolwork, attended all their games, took care of everything. Actually, she babied me, too. Carm wouldn't let me do any serious fixing around the house for fear I'd injure my hands—my livelihood. But she'd always set things straight.

If I came home grumpy from a bad game or something, she'd say, "You want problems? Let me tell you about my day."

Any marriage is a trust. It's a foundation on which a family is built. To this day, there's nothing in life I cherish more than Carm and our three boys—Larry, Tim, and Dale—and nine grandchildren. We're enormously proud of them. We remain a real close-knit family, and that's the way it's always been.

Carm's had a real good influence on me. She's given me the gift of good taste. When we go somewhere, I still ask her what I should be wearing, though I won't always take her advice. We're both strong-willed. We like to disagree sometimes. If I say, "Come on, Carm, we'll be late," she'll say, "Oh, Yogi, we can be late *once*." She can stay on my case pretty good.

Carm has a lot of interests, especially art, music, and theater, and is involved in too many charities for me to name. When I was playing, she was always organizing the Yankee wives for different causes. When the boys got older, she worked as a political researcher, and I always thought she would've made a good politician—well-spoken, smart, opinionated. Once we were invited to a state dinner at the White House by President Reagan, and Carm was seated with these big politicians, really holding her own. I was seated with the king of Saudi Arabia, and all we did was exchange autographs.

Hard to believe it's been more than half a century since I first met Carm. It was 1947, and I was just a nobody rookie with the Yankees. She was a pretty waitress in Biggie's restaurant in St. Louis. Finally, I got the nerve to ask her out. I wasn't the handsomest guy, but Carm said she liked me because I was honest, not a show-off. Through it all, it's been a great ride. Carm's been a great wife and we have a great time together, even when we're not.

I DON'T KNOW, I'M NOT IN SHAPE YET

As a rookie in 1947 in spring training, somewhere in Latin America. *Berra Archives*

I said this in spring training when someone asked what size cap I wore. Actually, people have always made fun of the way I'm built, short and blocky. I was five foot eight and about 192 pounds as a player, and looked even chunkier in a uniform. I wasn't exactly confused with Joe DiMaggio out there. But I always kept myself in shape—and still do. Plus my body was pretty deceptive, athletic-wise: I had good agility and was a pretty good runner. You can't do much about the way you're built—God determines that—but conditioning can go a long way in helping your performance and your confidence.

I was never a workout nut as a player. I wasn't big on weights or running long distances. We didn't have those "andro" things or muscle supplements these guys use today to bulk up. Truth is, I used to take a B-12 vitamin and had a healthy appetite. But as a player and a coach, I used to cut down on my eating—especially since I went to so many banquets—to keep my weight down and frequently would skip lunch. Now I'm an old-timer, but I stay in shape and feel pretty good by doing fairly regular exercise—golf, the treadmill, some light lifting—and by watching what I eat. I'm a creature of habit, so it's always a banana and bagel and coffee for breakfast. And I always look forward to a good dinner, plus my three ounces of vodka with ice. That's the most the doctor said I can have when he detected my irregular heartbeat a few years ago. I'm a bit obsessive about my one drink of the day. I truly cherish it.

You have to take your health seriously. Sometimes you lose sight of what's happening to your body because of stress or work. You stay at the office 'til eight o'clock, or you stay up too late worrying about money problems. Probably the worst I ever felt—mentally and physically—was when I was managing the Yankees in the 1980s. I was smoking more than I ever did. I was putting on weight. I was worried about things I shouldn't have worried about. When I got fired, it wasn't the worst thing that ever happened. I got to play golf more and that helped clear my head.

However, just before I turned seventy, I got the scare of my life. That was when my doctor found the arrhythmia during a checkup. From then on, I had to be monitored periodically. I had to take a blood thinner. I had to severely limit my drinking. I immediately quit smoking and started to seriously change the way I did things. And almost obsessively, I started working out. Along with my buddy John McMullen, I began a strenuous regimen at the New Jersey Devils' training facility and soon began to feel great, a bit lighter around the belt and much more energized. The only thing that wasn't feeling great was my right knee, which sometimes hurt like hell. All those years of squatting behind the plate finally took their toll—I needed a knee replacement.

At seventy-four years old, I got a new knee. Body-part replacements are modern miracles. But they only work if you make a real effort at rehabilitation—and the rehab is no cakewalk. You have to discipline yourself. The pain is absolutely excruciating at times. But I was so motivated to walk free and easy again, to play golf without pain, I pushed myself like I'd never pushed myself before.

I may be seventy-five, but I feel like I'm in great shape. I still get checked by the doctor, but my knee is great, I have good stamina, I'm still very active. And I've become more obsessive about food than Jenny Craig. Anytime someone offers me a pastry or a deli sandwich or whatever, I always have to find out the calories or if it's nonfattening. People are surprised to hear me ask that. But if you don't ask, you'll never find out. Anyway, I like the way my cap size fits now.

PUBLIC SPEAKING IS ONE OF THE BEST THINGS I HATE

Honored by my friends and neighbors on The Hill at Sportsman's Park in 1947. I was so nervous, I thanked everyone "for making this night necessary."
Berra Archives

The smoothest and most entertaining talker I ever met grew up right across the street from me. That's Joe Garagiola. I was the total opposite.

People say I have a way with words, but I look for the way out before speaking at a banquet or ceremony. Mickey Mantle, who also hated making speeches, said he'd almost rather face the electric chair. I know what he meant. I never got nervous playing in front of 50,000 people, but talking in front of them was a different story.

Early in my career, Joe was asked to present an award to me back home in St. Louis. He gave a big, long warm-up speech. When he finally gave me the award, I said, "Thanks," and sat back down.

I didn't do much better my rookie year, when the Yankees were in St. Louis and my friends from The Hill, the neighborhood I grew up in, had a night for me at Sportsman's Park. I was so nervous, I asked Bobby Brown, my teammate, to write me a short speech. I had it typed on a card—"I want to thank everyone who made this night possible"—and must have gone over it a thousand times.

But when the announcer called me to the microphone, I somehow said, "I want to thank everyone who made this night necessary."

I learned how to be a ballplayer, not a speaker. Lots of people have trouble with public speaking, so I can relate. It's not easy talking in front of strangers. I've just never been comfortable at it, not even after hundreds of banquets, dinners, and ceremonies. It's also worse because I can't memorize anything and I get kind of emotional sometimes. Anything that reminds me of family or The Hill, I get a little choked up. Don't ask why.

I guess a little emotion isn't bad, if you remember the speeches by the three greatest Yankees of all time. Lou Gehrig told a packed Yankee Stadium that he was the luckiest man on the face of the earth, even though he was real sick. And I was a young player near home plate at the Stadium when Babe Ruth, without much voice left, gave his farewell speech two months before he died. He gestured toward us and said, "The only real game in the world, I think, is baseball." I remember having tears in my eyes.

The next year, 1949, there was a special day for Joe DiMaggio, even though he was still playing and we were in the middle of a pennant race. Joe was extremely gracious, thanking everybody and even acknowledging the Red Sox, our opponent. Then he finished by saying, "I want to thank the good Lord for making me a Yankee."

Those guys all said it best. No script. Right from the heart. If you have to make a speech, that's really the only way to do it.

8

HE'S LEARNING ME ALL
HIS EXPERIENCE

With the great Bill Dickey, who "learned me all his experience." *Berra Archives*

You always hear about a player or a coach or a manager being called a "student of the game." That's a bit over-rated. Anybody who plays baseball or does anything else for a living—electrician, accountant, chef, mom—has to learn what to do. You get trained and prepared, then you get skilled. You always learn by doing, but you also learn by learning, if you know what I mean.

I learned baseball by instinct. Growing up, I was never really trained or coached. We never had Little League. I just did what felt right, even if it was swinging at a pitch at my shoetops or eyebrows. I had good natural ability as a hitter, but I never learned the fine points of catching. So when I was a young catcher in my first couple of years with the Yankees, I was clumsy and scatter-armed. My own pitchers had little confidence in me, and I couldn't blame them.

But I had the good fortune of playing for Casey Stengel. Casey was an instinctive genius—he had a great feel for things. He was a master at platooning. He was one of the first to show that the bench and bullpen were just as important as the starting lineup. He was also a great teacher.

When Casey became our manager in 1949, people laughed. He was almost sixty years old and still had a loser and clown image. But it was Casey who started shaping our championship teams . . . and my career. Casey had the foresight to see my future as a catcher, even though I was absolutely awful my first two years. I was so awful that Bucky Harris, our previous manager, had moved me to the outfield, where I wasn't as awful. At twenty-three, my career was at a crossroads.

Casey knew I needed serious help. He brought in Bill Dickey out of retirement to mold me into a catcher. Dickey was a great catcher for the Yankees in the 1930s—a Hall of Famer—and now I was his project. I had an awful lot to learn because I did everything wrong—throwing, footwork, mechanics, even my crouch was all wrong.

Each day for at least a couple of hours, Dickey worked with me. He worked me on all the details of catching: how to chase pop-ups, how to spot a batter's weakness, how to move my feet . . . everything. All the while, he worked on my confidence. He kept encouraging me, telling me, "Take pride in your position. It's the best job in baseball." He was also motivating by reminding me there weren't many good catchers, and that once I established myself I could have a great career. Dickey helped turned things around for me.

Looking back, I realize if I hadn't been tutored by Bill Dickey, I might not have lasted long in baseball. Who knows? I might've wound up back in the Johansen Shoe Company in St. Louis, where I worked as a teenager, pulling tacks out of shoes. I owe a great deal to Dickey. I've never forgotten him for "learning me all his experience." Yes, I did say that back in spring 1949, and I can see why it sounded funny. But all that counted was that Bill, as he put it, "awakened pride" in myself, and my catching.

Even when you get older, you should never be a know-it-all. You can always learn from someone else's experience. When I became a manager, I always listened to my coaches. I figured what's the use of having coaches if you can't use their opinions and experience? I'd always make the final decision, but I wanted their input. For years and years, Frank Crosetti was a great Yankee coach, a manager's coach. Serious as heck, but smart. He played when Ruth and Gehrig played. How can you not use all those smarts? I know some managers who barely talk to their coaches—maybe it's an ego thing. They act like they invented the game. That's not good.

Every young person should have a mentor. Students, businesspeople, even ballplayers. They need wisdom and experience. They need encouragement. They need someone who has been through it all. I've done and seen a lot, so I've always tried to give a little something back. When I saw the determination of a young kid like Don Mattingly, Craig Biggio, or Jorge Posada, I would go and talk to him and encourage him. Experience is a great thing—everyone can learn from it.

35

IF YOU DON'T HAVE A
BULLPEN, YOU GOT NOTHING

I got to manage my son Dale, briefly, as Yankee manager in 1985. I was gone after sixteen games. *Berra Archives*

Pitching is 90 percent of baseball. Maybe 75 percent. Or 65 percent. It depends on which "expert" you talk to. But it's still the most important part of the game. And bullpens—meaning relief pitchers—are more important now than ever.

I said you're nothing without a bullpen thirty years ago. That was before starting pitchers considered five or six innings "a quality start." And before relief pitching became so specialized—one pitcher coming in to face one batter, another coming in to face another, the closer only pitching the ninth. Call me old-fashioned, but I don't agree with that philosophy. I say, keep a guy in there if he keeps getting outs. Why remove someone if he's doing the job?

Bullpens and the people in them are real important. They're lifesavers. They get you out of trouble and make it possible for you to win. How you handle guys in the bullpen will tell a lot about your team's success. You need to be encouraging, even when they fail. You need good communication with them. Most important, you need good talent.

Nowadays bullpens are like most walks of life. You have a specific job and responsibility. You have to perform when called on. Now, you're either a long reliever (come in the game early when all is lost), a lefty or righty specialist (come in to face one or two hitters), a setup man (come in the seventh or eighth innings), or a closer (almost always pitching only the ninth inning). It's like a business, where you have a division of labor. But boy, I'd hate to be pigeonholed into one thing. I think it creates staleness. Casey Stengel always felt ballplayers should be versatile and able to play other positions. Why shouldn't businesspeople also have versatility and different skills? I'd think it would make them more valuable.

It seems everything's too specialized these days. Even baseball. Heck, we never had a designated hitter. Or so many specialty coaches. Or so many guys in the bullpen, setup men, long relievers . . . I think that's why you always have at least one unhappy guy in a bullpen. He knows he can do more, but he's been branded into one role.

Still, all relief pitchers face pressure. Usually when they come in, the game's in their hands. They must be tough. They must know how to handle crushing losses. As a catcher and a manager, I'd never get down on my relievers. Even after a loss, I'd always pat 'em on the back and say something encouraging. Always be reassuring when someone fails, because you may need them to perform tomorrow. Everybody has a bad day at the office or at home, the idea is to not dwell on it. The idea is to bounce back. That's what teammates are for. Pick him up, boost his confidence. Good bullpens—like any good team—are like a support group.

Funny, bullpens weren't a real big thing when I broke in. Relievers used to be washed-out starters. They weren't seen as so vital. They didn't get credit for "saves" the way they do now. They didn't get great respect. But we had Joe Page in the late 1940s, and he helped change that. Joe was probably the first relief pitcher who became a star rather than just a guy who couldn't start.

In the 1950s and '60s, relief pitchers became better appreciated. I remember when Luis Arroyo was always coming in to save games for us in 1961. Whitey Ford said, "I'll have a great season if Arroyo's arm holds out." When I managed the Mets, Sparky Anderson, who was managing the Reds, hated when I'd bring in Tug McGraw. He knew Tug was fearless and his team had little chance, so he'd make some I-give-up gesture toward me and I'd give him a thumb-nose right back—it was all in fun.

When I later managed the Yankees, I surprised a lot of people by switching Dave Righetti—a starter who pitched a no-hitter in 1983—to the bullpen the next year because we didn't have a bullpen. But we had to really sell it to Rags, because he had doubts. We told him it would be good for him and the team. To me, Rags is one of the truest team players.

Every organization needs team players. People you can always depend on. Like I say, you always have to make them feel good about themselves—even if it's the bullpen mop-up guy—because they're part of the backbone of your team. Bullpens are lifesavers. Without a bullpen, you're sunk.

10

IF PEOPLE DON'T WANT TO COME OUT TO THE PARK, NOBODY'S GOING TO STOP THEM

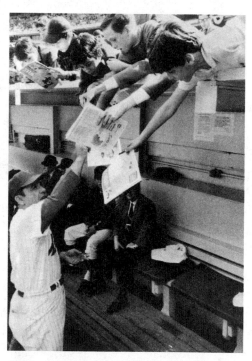

Signing autographs as a Mets coach in the mid–1960s. *Daily News*

I think I first said this about the poor attendance in Kansas City, when the A's were never too good. They eventually moved to Oakland in the mid-1960s. And I also said something like this to Bud Selig when he was interim commissioner. Attendance was declining in the early 1990s, and I think it was because of the threat of a strike.

The point is that you can't take anything for granted in baseball—or in business, or in life. Baseball's a great game, our national pastime and all, but you have to do a lot of things right to keep people coming to your games. Mostly, you have to win.

I always check the attendance of every box score every day, to see who's drawing, who's not. If a team's not drawing, they're usually losing. But it could also be because they play in an unattractive ballpark, or tickets are too expensive, the traffic and parking are bad, or they're just doing a bad job of making it easy for families to come.

As a kid on The Hill, I would occasionally go to Sportsman's Park to see the Cardinals or the Browns—the two major-league teams in St. Louis. I went as part of the Knothole Gang program, and we'd sit up in the left field stands. I'd like to see more kids' programs like that in the game today. Honestly, I rooted for both St. Louis teams. But looking back, the Cardinals were the big team, because they always had a winning season. The Browns were almost always losing. The Cardinals had colorful and exciting players, who captured our imaginations. Ducky Medwick, for one, was my idol. The Browns didn't have any real stars.

Bill Veeck, who was the game's greatest promoter, tried to change things when he bought the Browns. I liked Veeck. He was a real character. In my early years with the Yankees, I used to play cards with him in a St. Louis firehouse in the off-season. Veeck insisted he could draw fans even with a losing team through gimmicks and a carnival atmosphere. He tried, all right—remember, he brought in the midget and once had fans actually make managerial decisions in the stands. But the Browns kept losing and the fans stopped coming. He had to move the team to Baltimore in 1954.

A lot of fans stopped coming to the ballparks in the 1950s. That's why a number of other teams, like the Dodgers and Giants, also moved. People started moving to the suburbs, and most parks were hard to reach by car. Parking was limited. Television came in, and it was easier to stay home and watch.

Right now, I think there's more emphasis on the attractiveness of ballparks than ever. Now people need more than just to see a game—they need to see it in luxury and with all sorts of other activities going on. Things are more competitive now; there are more entertainment options. So teams feel they have to give people something other than baseball for their $45 ticket. That's too bad. Baseball is a great game. It doesn't need any sideshows.

People ask me all the time what I would do about Yankee Stadium. Many say it's too old (heck, it's older than me), it's got lousy amenities, and it's time for a new park. I know George Steinbrenner is unhappy with the neighborhood, the parking, the luxury boxes, and all that. But I'd keep it right where it is. Yankee Stadium is a shrine. It's got all that history. It's what people want to see when they come to New York, like the Statue of Liberty. I say the money would be better spent on the neighborhood and the roads around the Stadium. Then put in some new luxury boxes, too.

How bad can Yankee Stadium be? Sure, tickets are expensive and there's traffic, but nobody's stopping them from coming to the park. Over 3 million people in each of the last two years! Believe me, that ain't too shabby.

11

YOU CAN'T WIN ALL THE TIME. THERE ARE GUYS OUT THERE WHO ARE BETTER THAN YOU

Winning is contagious when you have big sticks on your side like Joe DiMaggio, Johnny Mize, and Charley Keller. *Archive Photos*

I've been real lucky, playing on great Yankee teams that won a lot of championships. I always was confident we'd win. So were my teammates. We all felt we could do whatever was necessary to win. And we won a lot. Winning those five straight championships, 1949–53, is a record. We had a good camaraderie on that team—we were like a family. But in sports or in anything, you can't win all the time. There's a thin line between winning and losing. You can get unlucky. You can have a bad day, or a bad quarter, or a bad fiscal year. Or face it, the team you're playing is better than yours.

I am a very competitive person. I don't like to lose at anything. Even now, whether it's playing gin with my buddies or a game of Monopoly with my grandkids, I'm totally intent on winning.

But I learned a long time ago that losing is a learning experience. It teaches you humility. It teaches you to work harder. It's also a powerful motivator. I've always said, somebody's got to win, somebody's got to lose. Accept the losses and learn from them.

Growing up in St. Louis, we'd play soccer in the fall and winter, and we lost all the time to teams from the Irish and German neighborhoods. They were simply better than us. But I think that losing in soccer helped make me more of a competitor. It made me hungrier to win. And I became more determined to improve my running and agility, which I did.

Most of the greatest competitors know how to win and lose graciously. I remember Jackie Robinson coming into our clubhouse after losing a tough World Series and congratulating us—he even gave me a hug. No matter how much you hated your opponent on the field—and the Brooklyn Dodgers and us had a ferocious rivalry—you always got along off it. Losing to us in the World Series must've been tough. But to me, the Dodgers were champs. I went barnstorming with guys like Pee Wee Reese and Roy Campanella in the off-season—we had fun. We got along great. When the Dodgers finally beat us in 1955, I teased Pee Wee that we let them win one. We didn't have Mickey Mantle or Hank Bauer, who were hurt. But no excuses. The Dodgers, especially guys like Johnny Podres, played great. They were better than us that year.

Sometimes your competitor is going to take your best client. Someone else at work might get the promotion. Your kid's soccer team might lose the championship. You have to accept the fact that some things aren't meant to be—like for us in '55. The Dodgers were due, they had such good ball clubs. When I managed the Yankees in 1964, we lost a real tough World Series to the Cardinals in seven games. I was pretty disappointed. But I went into their clubhouse to congratulate their manager, Johnny Keane. He knew I felt bad about losing and said his team got the better breaks. He congratulated me on a great series and said we put up a terrific battle. He said I should be proud, and that made me feel a little better.

I didn't feel too much better the next day when I got called into the Yankees' offices. I thought I was going to get a contract extension. I got fired instead. It was pretty shocking. We had won ninety-nine games, had a lot of injuries, and almost won the World Series. But I didn't want to sound like sour grapes—I told everyone I owed everything to the Yankees. I played seventeen wonderful years there; I had no regrets.

Getting fired is a strange feeling. It's hard. It's a big loss. But how you handle losing your job—or a game—is important. You have to move on. You have to look at the positives. For me, it was a great experience. I learned a lot about handling people in difficult circumstances. I felt I did the best I could. There's no shame in that.

Professional sports can be cruel, but youth sports shouldn't be. I see too much emphasis put on winning for young kids. Parents and coaches really need to teach kids that it's OK to lose, especially if you tried your best. Kids take their cue from adults. When they see their parents yelling at the umps or refs, it's a bad message. It takes the fun out of it. It also gives them an alibi when they lose. It doesn't teach them that losing is no disgrace.

Competition at all levels should be a good, healthy thing. I think you find out a lot about yourself as a competitor. Can you rise to meet a challenge? Do you take yourself too seriously? Can you congratulate whoever beat you? If you can't, something's wrong. Games are just that—games. If you don't win, face it. You just lost to somebody better. Shake their hand and try harder next time.

12

DON'T GET ME RIGHT,
I'M JUST ASKING

Putting on the "tools of ignorance." Funny, I always thought catchers were the smartest guys on the team. *Archive Photos*

Communication is real important in everything you do. It's probably never more so than today, where everybody's on cell phones or sending e-mail. But communication has always been a major part of baseball, where there's always signs and signals and just plain talking. As a catcher, I was one of two men on every play of the game and had to communicate all the time. I also did a lot of talking, reminding pitchers how to work the next hitter, chatting with umpires and fans, and talking to opposing hitters.

Funny, one of my pet peeves is people who gab too much. But I think I used my chattiness to my advantage. I made more friends in baseball by just being friendly and conversational. You're never going to get to know people if you don't talk to them. I got to know a lot of people that way. I wasn't being a jerk, talking on the field. I was just being me.

People say I always tried to rattle or distract the hitters, but that's not true. I would never talk during a pitch; that's bad sportsmanship. But I would usually pass the time during lulls between batters with anybody—the hitter, the umpire, the batboy, whoever. It gets lonesome behind the plate, so I appreciated the company. I didn't turn every at bat into a cocktail party, but I liked chitchatting, small talk, whatever. Maybe some of Casey Stengel, who could talk and talk, rubbed off on me. Casey used to say I said hello to everyone in sight, and that I was a very sociable fellow who acted like home plate was my room. But I think my banter helped my personality—it helped me overcome my shyness as a kid. It helped put an end to the insults I used to get early in my career.

I meant no harm in talking to batters. I just felt like talking. How's your wife? The kids? Getting in any golf? Stuff like that. Anything to be friendly and get his concentration a little off. I didn't talk to new guys right away. I had to find out about them first, and then find out if I could kid around with them. Truthfully, most guys didn't mind me talking. Only a few would get mad. Larry Doby, who now happens to be one of my best friends, used to hate when I'd try talking to him. Before I could even say, "How are you doing?" he'd tell the umpire, "Tell him to shut up." But I think that's because Larry was really serious and didn't want to hear any of my nonsense.

I would kid Vic Wertz about being bald. "Is that why you won't tip your cap to the customers, Vic?" When some guys said, "Yogi, don't talk to me," I'd say, "If you don't want me to, I'll never talk to you again." So they'd talk.

51

Ted Williams was as serious a hitter as there was, but he liked talking to me. We both used to kid around about pitchers and I would always talk to him about anything he was interested in, especially fishing.

On a rare occasion, I'd get on the nerves of an umpire. For some reason, I'd always forget and ask Tom Gorman about his family. Finally, he got tired of it and yelled at me, "My family died last night!"

The big thing is, I always had a good rapport with my pitchers. We learned to think along the same channels. That's what happens with good communication. Teamwork involves a good deal of talk between players and players and coaches—it's the same in any business. In baseball, as in business, you remind people of situations. You anticipate situations and discuss them. You tell people what you want done, even if they know it perfectly well. Reminders can't hurt. You write memos or letters or e-mails, you have meetings, you discuss goals. It's all about communication.

In baseball and business, good managers are good communicators. They let you know what they expect. Talking is a big part of any job. Late in my career, when I got switched to the outfield, it was easier on my knees, but I really didn't like it too much. Mainly because there was nobody to talk to.

13

IF YOU DON'T KNOW
WHERE YOU'RE GOING,
YOU MIGHT NOT GET THERE

With my brother John and Pop, who had told us how
rough it was crossing the Atlantic when he came from
the Old Country. *Berra Archives*

Nobody knows how life is going to turn out. Like so many roads I've gotten lost on, there are twists and turns and unforeseen circumstances. And exits you can't see well. But I learned that you can get to where you want to go if you know where you're going. What I mean is, you must have a good idea of what you want. You need a plan. You also need confidence and desire.

When I was about fourteen, my family and the parish priest were real worried about me. I was lousy in school. I didn't want to work. I wanted nothing more than to play sports. Pop was real frustrated with me—he didn't understand my obsession with playing sports all the time. All he saw was me playing on the streets, the school yard, and even a field we built on a garbage dump. When I'd come home dirty with torn pants, boy, would he get mad. It was finally agreed I would quit school in eighth grade to go to work. I guess Pop saw my future as a laborer, like him in the brickyards. Honest day's work, honest day's pay. I worked different jobs: on a Coca-Cola truck, in a shoe factory, at a coal yard. But I couldn't keep any of the jobs because I'd cut out and join my friends for a game.

I loved baseball. That's all I wanted to do. Pop didn't know baseball; he was from the Old Country. He didn't think you could make a decent living from it. My three older brothers, Tony, Mike, and John—who all would've been better than me if they didn't have to work to support the family—finally convinced Pop to give me a chance to become a professional ballplayer. My brothers never got their chance, but they knew how much it meant to me. I owe everything to them. Without my brothers, I never would've gotten the chance.

I knew what I wanted, which helped. I worked at it. I got pretty good at it. I was real fortunate to be a major-league player. But it did help that I had a good idea of what I wanted, so I could devote myself to that goal. And it helped that I got help from my brothers early on—that paved the way.

Not everyone knows where they'll wind up. School and college can help you find your interests—my situation was different. I was fixated on baseball pretty early, but I'm proud my sons and oldest grandchildren have gone to college. I think it helps that they have a realistic expectation of what they want to do. Career decisions are important. So is getting on the right road. Why take the trouble to go to law school unless you're certain you need to? Have a vision, a goal of what you want to do. Unless you're sure of where you want to go, you'll never get there.

14

NINETY PERCENT OF THE GAME IS HALF MENTAL

I was never a picture of grace or elegance,
but I pretended to be in this pose.
Archive Photos

Sometimes I speak in approximate percentages. It just happens. What I was saying is that baseball is a balance of physical and mental. Like anything, the mind and body are always linked. But since they say baseball is a thinking man's game, you have to use your brain a lot. Carlton Fisk, a real good catcher who was just inducted into the Hall of Fame, used to have a sign over his locker that said THINK. I bet that got his teammates thinking.

I was always thinking when I played, even if I did say you can't hit and think at the same time. That's only because you don't have time to think when a pitch is being thrown at you at ninety miles an hour.

To succeed in anything, you need good intuition and observation. It also helps to have a good memory. As a catcher, I used to study the opposing hitters: their tendencies, their weaknesses, their strengths. It goes to something I used to say as a manager: You can observe a lot by watching.

To me, there was always something in the way a batter stood, the way he held his bat, to tell you what pitch he was looking for. Always notice the little stuff, it helps.

I developed a good throwing arm and had a blocky body, which is good for a catcher. But I really used my brain more than anything. As a catcher, you scrounge for every edge. A thousand things happen in a game, little things, and you have to keep those things in your head. In the 1953 World Series, I threw two runners out at third base on back-to-back bunts. People thought I stole the Dodgers' signs. Truth is, I was watching how the batters' feet were pointed, and how our pitcher was keeping the ball where I wanted it. I could just tell the bunts were going to the left of the plate— and that's where they went.

You don't have to be a great world thinker or intellectual to use your head. You can be shrewd, if you pay attention. I used to call maybe 120 pitches a game—I had to be a little shrewd in mixing them up. As long as I can remember, I've always loved to play cards. And I used to play a form of gin rummy by keeping three columns of scores in my head. Believe me, I'm no magician—I just concentrated real good.

Being tough mentally can overcome a lot of physical pain. And you endure a lot of pain catching 150-plus games a year. To block out the discomfort, I just think about my task. Think that your teammates depend on you. Think that your experience can make the difference. Think that you're going to help the pitcher. Life is full of mind games. The trick is to try seeing yourself doing things you want to do—

that's positive thinking and concentration. Just try to avoid the strange mind games—like when catchers suddenly get mental blocks and can't throw the ball back to the pitcher. I guess that's caused by mental strain, but I'm not a psychologist, so I don't really know.

Funny, baseball seems more physical than ever now—everyone lifts weights and all the guys are much bigger and stronger. But the mental part may be more important. Now you see teams with their own psychologists, and players going to hypnotists. Even big, strong guys like Mark McGwire know that the game is more than half mental. I remember when McGwire was saying he was getting tired mentally, and he went and developed some visualizing techniques. It helped him concentrate better, and he started hitting home runs again. I believe he said, "The mind is power. Not everyone uses it." I think he's right.

15

WHY BUY GOOD LUGGAGE?
YOU ONLY USE IT WHEN
YOU TRAVEL

I was a bloody mess in 1957 when a foul ball car-
omed into my mask and fractured my nose. It actually helped my breathing. *Archive Photos*

Barnes & Noble, Inc.
19120 E 39th Street
Independence, MO 64057
816-795-9878 07-10-01 S02732 R004

When You Come to a Fork   10.17
0786867752
DISCOUNT   16.95 - 6.78

SUB TOTAL   10.17
SALES TAX   .68
TOTAL   10.85
AMOUNT TENDERED
CASH   20.00

TOTAL PAYMENT   20.00
CHANGE   9.15
Thanks for shopping at Barnes & Noble!
#137679 07-10-01 01:60P ALANA

Booksellers since 1873

Full refund issued for new and unread books and unopened music within 14 days with a receipt from any Barnes & Noble store.
Store Credit issued for new and unread books and unopened music after 14 days or without a sales receipt. Credit issued at lowest sale price.

Full refund issued for new and unread books and unopened music within 14 days with a receipt from any Barnes & Noble store.
Store Credit issued for new and unread books and unopened music after 14 days or without a sales receipt. Credit issued at lowest sale price.

No one has ever accused me of being extravagant. I'm not big on owning fancy things, and I'm not exactly what anyone would call flashy. Maybe my most prized possessions are my world championship rings, but I only wear one; Liberace I'm not. Heck, Carm and I don't even own an answering machine.

I've come a long way from being the son of immigrant parents who couldn't speak English. But I don't really think I've changed that much from being the kid on The Hill. Basically, I think you are what you are. Your values should never change. Family and church and sports—to me, that's always what meant the most.

People shouldn't forget where they came from. It should develop character. When I was twelve and helped organize the Stags A.C., we were the only team in our league that couldn't afford uniforms. That was real motivation for us to beat the other guys. I still take satisfaction in doing that.

I've never forgotten the struggle to get what I felt I deserved, especially during my early years in professional baseball. And especially in my contract battles with George Weiss, who was a pretty tightfisted guy. In 1949, a guy I knew who did my taxes gave me a form and asked what I expected to make. I told him it was none of his business—yet. Then he said, "Well, how much do you expect to be paid in 1949?" And I told him, "More than the Yankees expect to pay me."

I had a number of salary hassles with Weiss. After one season in the mid-1950s, I told him that I was going to be named the Most Valuable Player and should be paid like one. Weiss said that wasn't official—some of the newspapers said there were more valuable players than me. I told him that I read only the papers that said I was the most valuable. That's how it went with me and George.

By the time we moved to New Jersey, I finally reached a decent salary level and let Carm pick out a big house. We eventually gave it up when the boys grew up, and that was fine by me. I've always tried to keep life uncomplicated. All these years, I really haven't changed my temperament or way of life.

When I visit Yankee Stadium these days, I'm amazed by the luxuries for the players. They're millionaires; more power to them. But the impressive thing to me about guys like Paul O'Neill, Mariano Rivera, Bernie Williams, and

Derek Jeter is that they're great guys, very down to earth, very family-oriented. Success spoils, but I don't see that with these Yankees. Maybe these guys are rich and dress better than I do, but they seem to have a grip on what's important.

YOU CAN OBSERVE A LOT
BY WATCHING

Our gang on The Hill. That's Joe Garagiola at the
lower left, and me with the striped shirt in the middle.
Archive Photos

Things happen. Things change. It could be in a ball game, a classroom, a military camp, your boss's behavior, or your wife's mood. No matter what, it always pays to pay attention. You'd be surprised how much you can learn if you really keep an eye on things.

Here's what I mean. People were quite surprised when I was first named manager of the Yankees in 1964. I was thirty-eight years old and had been a player-coach the year before. But that's when Ralph Houk, our manager, came up to me in spring training and asked if I'd like to manage. "Manage who?" I asked. He said the Yankees. I was real flattered. But I had to keep it a secret the whole 1963 season because he didn't want anyone to know.

Ralph managed that last year before becoming the new general manager. So I decided I had to really observe everything that happened with the Yankees that year, watching how Ralph handled players and situations and trying to notice little things about my teammates I hadn't noticed before. I had to, because I'd be managing these guys the next season.

When I was announced as the manager after the '63 season, a reporter asked me what I had picked up from Casey Stengel and Ralph Houk, the two managers I'd mostly played for. I said, "You can observe a lot by watching."

And that pretty much has always been my philosophy. Even when I was a kid, I was known for watching things carefully. When I was playing American Legion ball, we didn't have benches or dugouts. So I sat with my arms and legs crossed, watching everything that was happening. One day, me, Bobby Hofman, and Jack Maguire—they were both on my team—came from the movies where we saw a travelogue about a Hindu guy who was called a yogi. The yogi sat with his arms and knees folded, like me. So they said I looked just like a yogi. Soon everyone called me Yogi—and they still do.

It's a good nickname, I guess. The thing is, I always observed a lot. Even Casey used to call me his "assistant manager" because I was always observing everything. He trusted me to go out and tell a pitcher what he might be doing wrong. As a catcher you do a lot of watching. You're the only player who faces his own teammates. You observe the mannerisms and tendencies of opposing hitters and the actions of your pitcher. Observing is learning. If you pay attention, you can learn a lot.

I think this is a good lesson in business, too. Companies spend a ton of money for consultants to spot the latest trends. But a lot of times, they just spot fads. Heck, you can save all that money by careful observation. Watch the stuff people buy. Learn about it, then keep track of it. You have to keep your eye on people if you want to know what's going to last or not.

To me, watching is serious business. I hate when people don't pay attention. When I was managing and a player asked me about something that happened earlier on, that bothered me. I'd say, "Watch the game!" or "Aren't you watching?" Even when I go to a game today, whether it's hockey or baseball or football, I don't like people talking to me when I'm watching. I'm quiet and intent. I'm observing.

You can observe a lot by watching, but I learned a long time ago it can also be risky. In World War II, I was on a six-man rocket boat headed for Omaha Beach during the D-Day invasion. Our job was to shoot at the German machine-gun emplacements so our guys could have a better chance of making it to the beach. With the bombs and flares in the sky, it looked like fireworks on the Fourth of July. It reminded me of the holiday back home in Forest Park. I didn't know enough to be scared, so I stuck my head out, just looking up at all the colors in the sky. I was apparently watching too much for my lieutenant, who yelled at me, "You better get your damn head down if you want to keep it!" I took his advice.

IT'S DÉJÀ VU
ALL OVER AGAIN

With Phil Rizzuto and Eddie Lopat, two great guys who were on our five straight world championship teams, 1949–53. *Archive Photos*

The 2000 Subway Series brought back a lot of memories. Half of the fourteen World Series I played in were New York–New York: we played the Brooklyn Dodgers six times and the New York Giants once. It was an exciting, glorious time. I think it was kind of a peak for baseball.

Baseball dominated the city. People were crazy for the three teams here from the late 1940s through the mid-1950s. There were ten newspapers in the city. We had the best teams here, the best fans anywhere. It was an unforgettable era, a great time to play baseball. And it was pretty amazing how successful we were. We had great guys, close-knit, like today's Yankees. The 2000 World Series reminded me a lot of those days. It's louder now, with the barrage of media and excitement and everything. But it was almost like déjà vu. Which, as you probably know, is a French term meaning "already seen," though I've mangled it into the phrase "déjà vu all over again."

Things do have a funny way of happening again—even if it takes a while, like a Subway Series. Who thought John Glenn would go into outer space, then do it again more than twenty-five years later? Scooters are the popular toys for kids again. There's a George Bush in the White House again. Forty years ago, it was *The $64,000 Question*. Today it's *Who Wants to Be a Millionaire?* Almost like déjà vu.

Before the Yankees played the Mets, it had been forty-four years since the last Subway Series. But you'd think I was still playing by the calls I got from newspaper, radio, and TV reporters. Everyone wanted to know what I remembered most about our Subway Series. What was the city like? Was there extra pressure? Did we hate the Dodgers? Did I ever think it would take so long for another Subway Series?

All I can say is it was fun. We didn't have to travel far. We just got on the bus at the Stadium and we were there in fifteen to twenty minutes. We played every day. The games took two hours, half the time of the games today. The season was over in early October. I'll tell you, we were thrilled to get to the World Series—we didn't really care who we played. Yes, it was sweeter beating the Dodgers, but it was even nicer getting that winner's share. Everyone thinks we always got a parade down Broadway, like they do now. Heck, we only got one parade—in 1947, my rookie year. That was a memorable season. It was baseball history—Jackie Robinson's first year. It was also the first Subway Series since World War II. It was the real beginning of our great rivalry with Brooklyn, and it was exciting as hell.

I wasn't married then, and lived in the Edison Hotel in Manhattan. I guess it was still the age of innocence. TV really hadn't come in yet. We didn't make big money, so we worked in the off-season. We were friendly with the fans. Things were simpler then. To get to one of the games in the '47 Series, Frank Shea, one of our pitchers, and I took the subway. Frank was kind of a comic and wore a mask. You couldn't help but feel that fun atmosphere all around—Brooklyn fans and Yankee fans always knew their baseball.

So many plays and memories stand out. People still talk about things that happened in those Subway Series. I still get asked about Jackie Robinson stealing home against us in 1955—I know he got called safe, but he was out. Guess the same will always go for Roger Clemens throwing that bat toward Mike Piazza—he said he didn't throw it intentionally at him, and I agree. People will argue that a long time, too. There's really nothing like a Subway Series for tension and excitement. The explosion of shouting at Yankee Stadium in the 2000 Series was the loudest I'd ever heard. It seemed just as loud at Shea Stadium, too.

My rooting interest? That's easy. The Yankees. I spent my whole playing career there. My ten years with the Mets as a coach and manager were good ones. I made a lot of good friends there, and I always want the Mets to do well. But I'm a Yankee.

When I was a kid, I rooted for both St. Louis teams—the Browns and the Cardinals. The only time they played against each other in the World Series was 1944 during World War II, and they called it the "Streetcar Series." I was about as far as you can be from St. Louis that year—I was in the Navy in North Africa. But I'll always remember listening to it on armed forces radio. The war depleted both teams, but that didn't matter. To me and everyone back home, the all–St. Louis series was a big deal.

There's no bigger deal than a World Series in New York. Especially when you win. Then you get the parade, which is an experience that's hard to describe. Hundreds of thousands of people, wall to wall, yelling, cheering, chanting, throwing confetti. Being named grand marshal of the parade this past year was a great honor. Carm and I drove in the backseat of a '52 Thunderbird, and the crowd was a sea of joy. Just unbelievable. Kids and even adults too young to have seen me play were chanting, "Yogi! . . . Yogi! . . . Yogi!" It was a warm feeling, it really was. It was great to be part of a real joyous celebration of baseball. I know for these Yankees, the parade and all those cheers are something they'll always remember and cherish. It makes them proud to be Yankees, to be the champions. Just like the old days—déjà vu all over again.

18

WE MADE TOO MANY WRONG MISTAKES

My sons Tim and Larry help me polish off some hardware. *UPI/Corbis*

Everyone makes mistakes. I've sure made my share. Avoidable ones, wrong ones, you name it. For example, when I was forty, I mistakenly came out of retirement to play four games with the Mets in 1965. Not a good thing. The team was lousy, and I was in lousy shape. It was more of a public relations thing than anything. But when I struck out three times in one game (I used to go a whole month without striking out), I knew it was a big mistake. I hung 'em up for good right after that.

In baseball and in life, your condition, confidence, and concentration affect your performance. But everyone makes mistakes. In baseball, like everything, mistakes are physical or mental. In tennis, they say "forced and unforced errors." I like to say there's mistakes—and there's wrong mistakes.

What I mean is that wrong mistakes are more serious, more avoidable, more costly. They're usually more mental than physical. I really think most car accidents are mental mistakes—not paying attention, even for a split second, is as wrong a mistake as you can make.

Politicians try to avoid making mistakes, but it's hard. They get tired. They say things wrong. Sometimes they can't help it. When George Bush was running for president in 1988, he quoted me by saying his goal was to avoid making wrong mistakes. His opponent, Michael Dukakis, made a big mistake during his campaign by wearing that helmet in a tank. I think he got bad advice. That was a wrong mistake.

In baseball, you also pay a price for mistakes. You usually get second-guessed, especially on mental mistakes. Sportswriters and announcers harp on it all the time. I guess the best way to avoid mistakes is by not making them. I was real proud that I once played 148 consecutive games without making an error—I think that's because I had good concentration. That helps avoid physical and mental letdowns.

When we played the Pittsburgh Pirates in the 1960 World Series, it was hard to believe we lost. It was real strange. We crushed their pitching. We won three of the games, 16–3, 10–0, and 12–0. We were the more experienced and stronger team. But we lost in a wild and weird Game 7 when Bill Mazeroski hit that homer in the ninth inning over my head in left field. To this day, I thought the ball was going to hit the fence. Anyway, when a reporter asked me later how we could lose to the Pirates, I said, "We made too many wrong mistakes."

And we did. Almost all were mental, too. In the eighth inning of Game 7, we were leading, 7–4. The Pirates were rallying when our pitcher, Jim Coates, forgot to cover first on Roberto Clemente's infield grounder. That was a mental mistake—it kept the inning alive, and Hal Smith followed with a three-run homer.

Another mistake people still talk about was our manager, Casey Stengel, not using Whitey Ford in the first game. Whitey was our best pitcher. But Casey used Art Ditmar instead, and Ditmar got hit pretty hard. Casey later admitted it was a mistake on his part, and it would eventually cost him. He got fired after the World Series.

There was talk that Casey was too old. Even he joked during the season that "most people my age are dead at the present time." But he was still a great manager. Seven championships in twelve years, that's pretty damn good. I think he was a little bitter about being fired. He knew he could still manage. But Casey knew the Yankee owners wanted a younger guy. He said it best when he said, "I'll never make the mistake of being seventy again."

19

LITTLE LEAGUE BASEBALL IS A GOOD THING BECAUSE IT KEEPS THE PARENTS OFF THE STREET AND THE KIDS OUT OF THE HOUSE

I had a happy childhood. That's Charlie Rivas on the left, me on top. We played every sport possible when we weren't just hanging out. *Berra Archives*

A lot of people ask me what I think about Little League. It's funny, because I never played it. We never had organized leagues or travel teams on The Hill. Everything was sandlot; just a bunch of kids playing. And it was always fun. We made our own rules and played by them. We played ball all the time, choosing up teams among ourselves, playing barefoot, drawing the foul lines, putting nails in cracked bats, and crushing cartons for bases. We even created the 1930s equivalent of a Little League ball field on the neighborhood garbage dump and actually made dugouts out of two wrecked cars. Our games were like the way the kids now play in Latin America—finding whatever they can just to play because they love to. We had a passion for the game. We played all day long and, boy, we had fun.

Little League should always be about having fun. I'm real big on kids playing sports, because I think it's healthy and teaches teamwork and respect. Little League is good in that way. Like Babe Ruth said, baseball is a game you start young and have to keep practicing and playing. That's true for any sport. It's too bad, though, that many kids don't play ball now unless they're given uniforms, coaches, trophies, and banquets. I guess times change.

But Little League can be a great experience for kids, as long as they want to play—and don't play to bring their parents glory. The charm of baseball is that it's a kid's game. Good coaches and parents can have a positive influence. They can boost confidence. They can reinforce the importance of teamwork. They can help kids deal with failure. But I've seen too many of my grandson's games when kids feel unnecessary pressure. Like when they strike out and then look up at their parents as if they did something terrible.

The thing is, if a kid isn't having fun in Little League, he shouldn't be in it. I would like to see the essence of sandlot ball somehow be put into Little League. A kid shouldn't feel like it's the end of the world if a ball goes through his legs. He or she should laugh it off, like we used to. Each kid should be having a great time playing ball; no cares in the world. As a father, I hardly ever got to see Larry, Tim, and Dale play Little League. I always had my own games, but I know they didn't miss me. They had fun playing and would keep playing ball with their friends when their games were over. You don't see a lot of that today.

A lot of people think Larry, Tim, and Dale became good athletes because of me. Kids would always say to them, "You're good because your dad teaches you stuff all the time." That's wrong. I wasn't around that much in baseball season—I scarcely even saw their games. When I'd come home and they'd ask me to have a catch, I'd say, "That's what you have brothers for." And that's what they did, play ball with their brothers, their friends, themselves, because it was fun.

When I was playing with the Yankees, I'd drive past the sandlot field next to Yankee Stadium, and it was always filled with kids. They'd wave, "Hi Yog," but would never stop playing. Looking back, there's a good chance one of those skinny kids was Rod Carew, who used to play there a lot and was scouted off the sandlots of the Bronx. Those kids were having a great time, and it was great to see.

But today, when I go past that same field, it's always empty. Nobody's playing. Whatever kids are around are the ones behind the fence by the Stadium entrance, waiting five, six hours for an autograph. That's kind of a shame. Participation in Little League has gone down, and you wonder why. Is soccer more popular for kids? Basketball? Is Little League really a fun experience for kids?

I will say that when Little League baseball is done right, when the coaches and parents just let the kids play and enjoy themselves, it's one of the best things for a kid's childhood. I'll never forget meeting the 1998 Toms River Little League world champions—they were special. After they did a TV show in New York, they came to our museum, which at the time was just concrete and steel beams. Some of the parents and coaches wanted them to meet me, even though many of the kids had never heard of me. "We're going to see Yogi Bear?" one of them asked.

Well, I had followed them during the Little League tournament. They were just eleven and twelve years old, but you could see the joy and passion they had for the game. And their innocence. They were having a great time playing ball. And the coach, Mike Gaynor, he was great. He actually cut the number of kids on his roster so nobody had to sit and no parents could complain. He just wanted the kids to play and enjoy it.

When the kids gathered around where the museum was still unfinished, I was asked to say a few words. I looked at the kids in their baseball uniforms and kind of saw my childhood rushing back. I told them that I didn't have Little League as a kid, but I loved to play ball, just like they did. I told them I was so proud of the way they acted. I told them their passion for baseball reminded me of when I was their age. I actually got a lump in my throat and even became a little teary-eyed when I looked at their faces. I could see how much baseball meant to them. I wanted them to know how much it meant to me. "If I had to do it all over again," I told them, "I'd do it all again."

20

A NICKEL AIN'T WORTH
A DIME ANYMORE

Making Mom and Pop proud was real important to me. *The Sporting News*

You don't need to be a financial expert to know the importance of money. It's hard enough making money, and it's hard to make the most of it. I learned that growing up on The Hill, a neighborhood of Italian immigrants in the southwestern part of St. Louis. My father worked in the brickyards and didn't have it too easy. He had a wife and five kids to support on a laborer's pay. Money for the things the family needed and the things us kids wanted was something you had to think about all the time.

As soon as my three brothers and I were old enough, we had to hunt for jobs to help support the house. Working cost my brothers Tony and Mike their education and a chance to play organized baseball. But they did what they had to do.

As kids, we were always scheming to get loose money. My friends and I would find customers who needed manure for fertilizer, and we'd carry bags for a nickel or a dime. I'd sell newspapers for three cents. Joe Medwick, who became my idol, was my best customer because he'd give me a nickel. And when I was thirteen, I got into a boxing club and got paid five or ten bucks a fight. I always gave the money to Mom. Before the club folded, I fought nine times, winning eight of them. Mom and Pop knew about it but didn't care as long as I didn't get hurt.

Actually, sports was the only real outlet for kids on The Hill. Joe Garagiola and I played every sport there was—softball, corkball, baseball, soccer, roller hockey. But Pop didn't like me playing ball. He hated me coming home with dirty pants. And he'd give me a smack if they were torn, since we couldn't exactly afford new ones.

So I grew up knowing money didn't come easy. I came to appreciate it a lot. I learned to be stubborn with money. I learned my own worth. I always figured I wanted to play baseball more than anything in the world, and still get paid what's coming to me for it. People always said that I'd play for nothing if I had to. I'm not saying I would or wouldn't, but I don't think that has anything to do with it.

Sure, I loved to play. And once I signed my contract, I forgot about the money and just concentrated on the game. But I made up my mind that I should get whatever I was worth. I felt I proved myself to the Yankees. If you're a valuable part of an organization, you should get a fair price. And you should say so. Nobody's going to go to bat for you unless you do it yourself. We didn't have agents when I played. I just made my case to George Weiss, our general manager, and asked for what I thought was fair.

Standing firm is important. I learned that after a couple of painful lessons. I had some pretty hard contract battles with Weiss, and he was tough. But I learned that whenever you negotiate, you should leave room for compromise, yet still stick to your guns. Don't let anyone take advantage of you. Use whatever leverage you have. Don't sell yourself short. This is true in business and in any aspect of life when you need to negotiate.

When we were sixteen, Joe Garagiola and I had a tryout with the St. Louis Cardinals. Branch Rickey, the general manager, offered Joe a $500 bonus to sign. The best he offered me was $250. I wanted what Joe got, and I felt I was worth it. So I didn't sign. I went back to work, then joined American Legion ball. The next year, John Schulte, who was a Yankee scout, told George Weiss that I was worth the $500. So I signed with the Yankees and reported to Norfolk of the Piedmont League in 1943. But they kind of pulled a fast one on me. My salary was $90 a month, and I wouldn't get the $500 unless I lasted the season there. Worse, I didn't have enough money to live on in a military town with the war going on.

I had to write home and ask Mom to send me money to eat. She warned me not to ever let Pop know, or he'd order me to come home. Once I went on a sitdown strike—I told our manager in Norfolk, Shaky Kain, I was too hungry to play. He fished out a few bucks and I went out and got some hamburgers and Cokes, then returned to play.

Like I said, my early contract battles with the Yankees and

George Weiss were beauts. Remember, I was making only $12,000 after I got married in 1949. And we had won the World Series that year. The Yankees offered me a $4,000 raise, which I didn't think was right. I sent them a note back saying I wanted $22,000, though Carm and I agreed we would take $18,000.

Funny, when reporters asked me if I'd seen the Yankees' first contract offer, I didn't want people to know, so I said I hadn't even opened the mailed contract. They said, "You mean you didn't even look at it?" And I said, "Nope, I knew it wasn't enough so I just told Carm to mail it right back to them." I thought Weiss would understand that I meant that I shouldn't talk about it, but he got pretty mad instead. We finally hashed it out in person, back and forth. I finally told him I was tired of fighting with him and that he ought to let me talk to the owners. I think that broke him down. He offered me $18,000, and I took it.

My highest salary as a ballplayer was $65,000. But I always supplemented my income with good investments— like the bowling alley Phil Rizzuto and I owned, and the Yoo-Hoo Chocolate Drink Company, of which I became a vice president. I've been very fortunate to earn a good living and live in a nice house. I've been comfortable, and that's more important to me than all the money in the world. But my early experiences shaped me. To this day, I'll always conserve. I turn out the lights in a room right after I leave. I'll always price different things before I buy.

People always saw me as easygoing and naive, but I was

tough and stubborn when it came to money. I was determined to get what was due me at contract time. I never forgot that shabby treatment when I was starting out. I guess I've always been serious about money. Maybe because it was hard to get, and it's never worth what it once was.

21

IT AIN'T OVER 'TIL
IT'S OVER

As a coach with the Yankees in the early
1980s, I appreciated the good wishes.
© Yvonne Hemsey/Liaison

I don't think there's a truer lesson in life. Never assume anything's really finished or officially happened . . . until it's really finished or officially happened. It can be a ball game or a closing on a new house. It can be a war or an election. It's like they tell you as a kid—don't count your chickens before they hatch.

I've always lived by this rule, especially when things look darkest. It's a great thing to tell yourself when you don't get what you want most. Nobody ever wanted to be a major-league ballplayer more than me. When Branch Rickey told me at age sixteen after a tryout with the Cardinals, my hometown team, that I was too awkward and should find another career, I was pretty brokenhearted. Coming from the smartest man in baseball, it was real discouraging. But I couldn't accept that my baseball career—my great hope—was over before it started. I reminded myself that I was still young. I could improve by keeping on playing, which I did in American Legion ball, and eventually I'd get another chance. And I did when I got signed by the Yankees in 1943 to play for their minor-league team in Norfolk.

I know politicians like to say it ain't over 'til it's over, because it gives them hope. That's good. They should be positive and keep their supporters hopeful. My mom and pop and all the Italian families on The Hill were big on Harry Truman. They liked him because he was a Democrat and for the common man, and not afraid to speak his mind. And he always was optimistic, despite people telling him he couldn't win. "I wonder how far Moses would have gone if he'd taken a poll in Egypt?" he used to say. The newspaper that ran the headline "Dewey Wins" proved that the election really wasn't over until the last votes were counted. Then it was over.

The 2000 presidential election was a dandy, too. The election was over, but it wasn't. At least for a long time, until all the recounts and courts got into it. To be honest, I didn't think I'd ever hear "It ain't over 'til it's over" so much in a political race.

A lot of people think I said, "It's not over until the fat lady sings," but it wasn't me. It was Dick Motta, who used to coach the Washington Bullets in the 1970s. His favorite saying was, "The opera isn't over until the fat lady sings," so when things didn't look good for his team, he'd tell everyone to wait for the fat lady. I guess he was saying everything has to run its proper course.

That's what I learned about baseball. It's a long haul. The season is played out day by day, night by night, and that's why the game has timeless appeal. No matter how terrible things look, you have a chance for a great redemption at the end . . . if you believe you can do it.

Just look at the Mets in 1973. I was managing them, but we were going downhill fast. We were in last place in mid-August. Some of our key guys were injured. The newspapers all said I was going to get fired. There was even a magazine article that came out called "The Last Days of Yogi Berra." I think the owner, M. Donald Grant, couldn't wait to bring in a new manager. But I tried to keep a brave face on things. I didn't want the players to think I was panicky or worried. I just tried to sound hopeful and realistic. And patient.

I told the reporters that the other teams had had their hot streak, and we were due for ours. Yes, I was frustrated pretty bad during that season. But I never lost faith in the players and would talk to each individually to keep their spirits up. I remember Cleon Jones was hurting pretty good, but he was our best offensive player. I told him if he gave everything he had, he could still carry us. I don't really believe in pep talks. Professional athletes should motivate themselves—if they have any pride. But everybody can use a pat on the back or a "hang in there" when things aren't going well. And if we lost a close game and things started to look bad again, I said, "It ain't over 'til it's over." I didn't want our guys to give up.

I think eventually even the players began to feed off that. Tug McGraw, our best relief pitcher, was having a terrible year. But one day in late August, he was trying to get the guys to think positive and kept saying, "You gotta believe." That was kind of our rallying cry in the last month, and we went on to win the pennant.

When I was a coach with the Yankees in 1978, we were trailing the Red Sox all year—and were still behind in the last month. But I felt we were starting to get hot and could catch them. George Steinbrenner, who was a real worrier, didn't believe it. So I made a bet with him—he'd give me a Cadillac if we won; I'd give him free membership in our racquetball club if we didn't catch Boston. I'm really not a gambling man, but I wanted to make the point that anything can happen if you play hard to the end. And the Yankees did just that. We eventually beat the Red Sox on Bucky Dent's homer in a playoff. Instead of the Cadillac, Carm asked for the money that would've bought the car and donated it to the theater company in our town.

Baseball history is full of great comebacks. I think that's a great lesson in life. Be calm, be patient, don't overworry. Good things can happen if you persevere. Nothing's final or official until it's final or official. Or as Jim Murray, the old sportswriter, used to say: "When you think everything is hopeless, just remember Yogi Berra."

22

IT GETS LATE EARLY
OUT HERE

I'm real close with my nine grandchildren.
Gretchen, who's now in college, once helped me
deliver potatoes to a food shelter.
© *Yvonne Hemsey/Liaison*

Toward the end of my career, I played a good amount of games in left field. This was a tough place to play in Yankee Stadium during the World Series because the autumn sun cast deep shadows across the field. When I said, "It gets late early out here," people laughed. But someone told me there's truth to that quote for older people—your later years come earlier than you expect.

I have to admit that's true. I got to be a senior citizen before I knew it. When I left baseball at age sixty-four, things didn't seriously change all that much. Sure I missed the camaraderie of the players and coaches. But I got to play more golf, and that's a good social thing. I got to see more friends. I stayed active. I exercised. I traveled. I still felt young, despite some creaky knees.

I still feel pretty good for an old-timer. Health care, surgeries, and therapies have never been better. No question that's helped me. And as Donna Shalala, the former secretary of health and human services (and a big Yankee fan), said, "There's never been a better time to be older than today." Older people are the fastest-growing population in the country. We're finding new ways to live longer and still be productive.

Phil Rizzuto, who's now eighty-something, told me that his seventies were the best ten years of his life. He said he really enjoyed life being older. And this from a guy who was supposed to be a hypochondriac and worrier when he was young.

I've been fortunate to be near my family. I see my nine grandkids a lot. I still do many things with my sons. Too many older people grow more apart from their families, or maybe it's the other way around. That's sad. I can tell you that being around kids, being part of their lives, keeps me feeling young.

It's good to see older people going back to work. They have skills. They have a lot to contribute. I enjoy going to spring training with the Yankees and helping out whenever they ask. I still have something to offer—it feels good when the players ask me things. Age shouldn't affect your thinking. Tommy Lasorda was still as enthusiastic and positive as ever when he managed our Olympic team to the gold medal in Australia. You'd never know he was seventy-three.

I get a kick out of seeing guys like Arnold Palmer still amaze people with their skills. The people who go into the Senior Olympics—some of them are over eighty—are amazing. This is sort of a golden age for older people. It's a great time to travel, to do the things you want. I think it's important to keep busy, enjoy your family, and set goals. It's a good time to help others. I do a lot of charities, and it's a good feeling when you give back and help people who need it. I also think it's important to listen to older people, hear their advice—and take it.

The frustrating part of getting older is slowing down physically. Things happen to your body. I'm glad my sons talked me into getting knee replacement surgery. It's helped me stay active. Put faith in your doctors. And keep track of yourself. If you're smoking or drinking too much or eating wrong, your body will tell you.

Back when I was in my mid-thirties, my body started telling me that catching was wearing me down. That's why Casey put me in the outfield to keep me in the lineup. It added years to my career. Like I say, my later years came earlier than I expected. But even though I'm retired now, I still set goals. Because if you don't set goals, you can't regret not reaching them.

23

IF YOU CAN'T IMITATE HIM,
DON'T COPY HIM

I owe everything to my family, who allowed me to pursue my dream of playing baseball. *Top row,* brothers John and Mike, mother Paulina, and brother Tony. *Front row,* sister Josie, father Pietro, and me as a nine-year-old. *Berra Archives*

You should always be true to yourself. Be your own person. It's OK to idolize somebody—Joe Medwick was my hero and favorite player as a kid—but you have to do things that feel right for you. Whether it's baseball or golf or any activity, it takes a lot of practice to find your own style, your own identity. Don't try to be somebody you're not.

By the same token, I think role models are very important to kids. Good role models set good examples. They can make a difference. If I had any role models, they were probably my three older brothers, John, Mike, and Tony. They were dutiful sons—they always gave their earnings back to the household—and had a real good work ethic. And they were also real good ballplayers. Tony, who was called Lefty, was the best ballplayer in our family, but he couldn't do anything with it beyond semi-pro. When he was offered a tryout with the Cleveland Indians, Pop wouldn't hear of it.

But mostly I learned a lot about respect from my brothers. I learned how to conduct myself, how to care about others. They helped teach me to be a good person. Because they went out on a limb and pleaded with Pop to give me a chance to play baseball when they weren't allowed to, I remain forever grateful to them. I badly wanted to make them proud.

Being a good role model means living a positive life, taking care of your family, and doing good for society. Being in the public eye carries a certain responsibility—whether athletes or celebrities like it or not, they are role models. That means they should be making a difference in people's lives, they should be responsible. I get disappointed when a player acts like a bad citizen and does crazy stuff off the field.

But the majority of role models aren't famous people—they're regular everyday mothers and fathers. They obey the law. They do important jobs. They contribute to society. They're living positive lives and are the most important role models kids can have.

It's too easy for kids to admire and try to copy famous people. Truth is, they're pretty much told to. Michael Jordan was the best basketball player in the world, and those commercials told kids to "Be like Mike." Tiger Woods is the best golfer in the world, and you see all these different kids saying, "I'm Tiger Woods." Maybe I'm missing something, but shouldn't kids just be themselves?

I know both Michael and Tiger, and they're real great guys. And they had great role models—their fathers. I couldn't imagine their fathers ever telling them to be like somebody else. Their fathers were responsive to them, and reassuring. And they allowed their sons' natural curiosity and ability to take hold. Just like Derek Jeter. I got to meet Jete's parents and immediately could tell why he's such a great kid. I know Dr. Jeter taught his son to be himself and encouraged him to play sports with passion and confidence. The way he conducts himself off the field is a good reflection of his parents.

It's hard to appreciate how guys like Jeter have such an influence on young kids. But they do. I've seen kids who do all of Jeter's mannerisms on the field, all his little routines. Everybody's always imitating somebody. Heck, I've even seen Little League kids who can't really play, but they spit like champions.

I don't think it matters what you do in life; just do it in your own style. Be yourself. When I was a coach and hitting instructor with the Mets in the late 1960s, Ron Swoboda, a big, strong kid we used to call "Rocky," asked me for some advice. He said that if he stood closer to the plate, he thought he'd be able to handle the outside pitch better. I told him the pitchers would jam him instead. Then Swoboda started to disagree with me. "But Frank Robinson does it and they don't jam him," he said.

"That's because he's Frank Robinson and you're you," I said. "That's his style of hitting. If you can't imitate him, don't copy him."

24

IF I DIDN'T WAKE UP,
I'D STILL BE SLEEPING

I guess it was a long time coming. George Steinbrenner and I made our peace at my museum in 1999.
© *Arthur Krasinsky*

I'm more early bird than night owl. It's always been that way ever since I was a kid. Even during my playing days, I didn't spend a whole lot of time nightclubbing. At least not like Whitey, Mickey, and Billy did. I loved Mickey, but anybody who roomed with him said he took five years off his career. Anyway, my whole life I've been an early riser— I always get up at 6 A.M. no matter what time it is.

Actually, getting up early and being early is sort of my obsession. I have little patience with people who are late. And I'm always early for everywhere I have to be. My family laughs at how I'm so preoccupied by my daily calendar, my appointments, my travel arrangements, and the weather. My sons say I'm the most regimented person on the planet. That may be true, but at least I'm never late.

When I was with the Yankees, I was always one of the first ones at the ballpark. In my rookie year, 1947, we had an exhibition game at Ebbets Field, and I was so worried about taking the wrong train that I left an extra hour early. Being early to all our games became important to me. I'd bone up on the opposing team, read the papers, get treated in the training room, shoot the breeze with the guys, do everything to get ready for the game. Casey Stengel used to joke I was just trying to get out of the house early and leave the kids with Carmen. But even when the kids were grown, I'd get to the ballpark way before the others.

Being a major-league ballplayer was a great time in my life. I had every reason for being happy and useful, and I wanted to do everything to make the most of it. Being early and being prepared—to me, that was a big part of doing my job.

I've learned that bad things can happen, and often do, when you leave things to chance. Usually, you're late. So I'll always leave extra early just to avoid traffic. To me, making people wait for you gives a bad impression. Just like being early or on time shows respect. Anybody who keeps me waiting, even if it's for a few minutes, they know I'll give them grief.

It's almost like when George Steinbrenner flew up from Tampa to come to my museum in New Jersey to apologize and make peace with me. We hadn't talked in fourteen years. It was a cold, winter day, and I heard that George was supposed to arrive at 5 P.M. When he showed up, he was kind of nervous about the whole thing. It was a few minutes after five. I looked at my watch, then looked at George.

My first words were, "You're late." I think he remembered my obsession for punctuality. We laughed, and that kind of broke the ice.

The importance of being prompt was instilled in me early. As kids, Joe Garagiola and I would get up at the crack of dawn on weekends to hold the field on The Hill. When our friends came, we were guaranteed a whole day of baseball.

During the week, the factory whistle would blow at 4:30 in the afternoon—quitting time in the brickyard. That meant Pop would be home in fifteen minutes. And that meant I'd better get over to Fassi's, the corner tavern, and get a bucket of beer filled and rush home so it'd be on the table when Pop got there. Believe me, no matter what game I was playing, I'd drop everything when that whistle blew. You didn't want to be late for Pop. You didn't want the consequences.

Actually, my early habits cost me a few roommates with the Yankees. Phil Rizzuto complained he lost too much sleep with me getting up so early. When Phil got another roommate, I was given Whitey Ford, with the idea being we could go over hitters together at night. But I don't think I helped Whitey, who was just a kid, all that much. Besides, he was usually doing other activities at night. Once in Chicago, when Whitey was supposed to pitch, we agreed to have breakfast together. I got up early, as usual. When Whitey asked me what time it was, I told him it was seven o'clock. So Whitey said, "The hell with breakfast. Wake me up at ten o'clock."

I had breakfast, then forgot all about Whitey . . . until I was at the ballpark having batting practice. Whitey was nowhere to be seen. I had a strange hunch he was still sleeping—and he was. Someone scurried to find a phone and woke him at the hotel. Twenty minutes before the start of the game, Whitey hurriedly arrived at Comiskey Park, then had ten minutes to get into his uniform and warm up. Casey Stengel and some of the veterans were pretty steamed. They thought Whitey was a young wise guy who wouldn't be long for a team that expected you to be your best. Believe me, Whitey was nervous as hell that game. Fortunately, we won and he was never late for the ballpark again.

NOBODY GOES THERE
ANYMORE. IT'S TOO CROWDED

Phil Rizzuto *(left)* and I sold suits in a
Newark clothing store after the 1951 season,
when I won my first MVP award.
Daily News

If you run a business, you can't overlook anything. You have to be hands-on, making sure everything's in order, making sure the customers are content, and making sure they want to come back. Their impressions become your reputation.

I learned a lot about keeping customers happy early in my baseball career, when I worked during the winter as a head waiter at Ruggeri's, a popular restaurant on The Hill. Henry Ruggeri, the owner, was a great guy. My brother John and Mickey Garagiola, Joe's older brother, worked there for years. But Henry always made you feel at home there—especially his loyal old-timers. He used to clear a special place for them at the bar when they just came in for a drink. He made them feel like neighbors.

Ruggeri's was a nice place; it was a good steakhouse with good Italian food. It had a friendly atmosphere. I wasn't the greatest greeter in the world, but I wanted people to feel comfortable there. Once I overheard a young couple getting nervous about the restaurant's style, saying they felt out of place. I went over and told them to relax, that after they'd been here ten minutes they'd think it wasn't any different from any neighborhood joint.

Later on, Ruggeri's was a place I'd bring my Yankee teammates whenever we were in St. Louis. I'd always go there with friends. At a certain point, I guess I stopped recognizing the regulars there and said, "Nobody goes there anymore, it's always too crowded."

I know that sounds kind of silly, but I think there's truth to it. Especially for businesses that cut back on their service. A lot of people are unhappy about the airlines because they delay and cancel flights more these days. People want good prices, they want a lot of choices, but mostly they want reliability.

When your name is attached to something, you'd better do what you can to make it good. Everything reflects on you, even if it's not always your fault. When Phil Rizzuto and I opened the Rizzuto-Berra Bowling Lanes in 1958, we took a personal involvement in the operations. We brought our brothers in to manage the place, and they kept it spotless. We had forty lanes, a real nice cocktail lounge and restaurant, and a nursery for kids. I even tended bar there occasionally and would bowl with the customers. It was a real good place and we had a lot of success there for years before we sold it. Same with our racquetball club that my son Tim managed. I was adamant it was always clean and first-class. People were surprised to see me hand out towels at times, but I felt a responsibility to make sure the members were satisfied. I've seen too many athletes lend their names to something that only becomes an embarrassment.

Just a couple of years ago, the mayor of Paterson, New Jersey, where Larry Doby grew up, renamed a ball field in a playground after him. There was a ceremony, with the mayor sounding proud as can be. But Larry wanted to make sure he wasn't going to be embarrassed. He said he was indeed honored. But then he warned the mayor: Unless he fixed up the field and maintained it, he'd take his name right off.

Now there's a minor-league stadium in my name at Montclair State, and they do a good job of keeping the field in great shape. The park is nice and intimate; it seats about 3,800. I like it that kids and families go to the games and have a good time. The hard part is getting them to come back again and again, especially when the team's doing bad. It's not just enough to have a great product, you need to find ways to reinforce customer loyalty. Any business has to remember this key point. If you don't do that, nobody will go there anymore.

26

SO I'M UGLY. SO WHAT?
I DON'T HIT WITH MY FACE

I've always said I was proud to be a major-
league player, and proud to be a Yankee.
Berra Archives

I'm not the greatest looking person in the world. Neither was Abraham Lincoln. My point? The way you look shouldn't affect what you do in life. If people want to laugh at you, ignore them. Or just laugh along. As Lincoln used to say, "If people say I'm two-faced, why would I use this one?"

In my early years with the Yankees, I took a lot of heat for my appearance. They said my looks improved when I put my mask on. I was called "The Ape." Someone said I had "a face like a fallen soufflé." When Larry MacPhail, my first general manager with the Yankees, first saw me, he said I resembled the "bottom man of an unemployed acrobatic team." That wasn't even the worst of it.

I got laughed at and mocked pretty good by the writers, the fans, even my own manager and teammates. I guess I made an interesting impression because I looked like an oddball—I was stumpy, and my clothes didn't fit real good.

Ted Williams always likes telling about the first time he saw me: "Who the hell are the Yankees trying to fool with this guy?" Reporters had a field day with my looks and mannerisms and would twist or exaggerate things about me. I didn't look like a major-league ballplayer, especially a New York Yankee, so I guess I was an easy target.

The more vicious stuff kept up pretty good my first few years. But I kept my feelings to myself. You just absorb it. Some of the stuff bothered me, but I really didn't mind. Basically I didn't want the jokes and insults to ruin my opportunity to play. There was more attention on me and that kind of made me more determined. I used some of the insults to play harder.

Being personally ridiculed is a test of character. You can't bury your head. Take it in stride. It may hurt underneath, but you can't let that stuff affect your attitude or performance. After a while, when I was asked about my looks, my stock answer was, "It doesn't matter if you're ugly in this racket. All you have to do is hit the ball, and I never saw anyone hit with his face."

Looking back, the insults weren't nearly as bad as the abuse that Jackie Robinson and Larry Doby took. They had the real hardship. They went through hell, just because of their skin color. They were black ballplayers trying to integrate baseball, when the whole country wasn't even integrated. The three of us all broke in the same season— 1947—but I played against Jackie in Montreal the year before, and he endured an awful lot. I think he pretended not to hear all the racial abuse, and he didn't say anything about his own teammates being chilly toward him. But I know it took a toll on him. It got worse when he joined the Dodgers. He ignored all of the slurs and taunts and had an intense desire to succeed. Same with Doby. They ignored all the abuse. They had no other choice.

Turning the other cheek is easier said than done, especially with abuse thrown at you. Think about how many fights are caused by someone simply saying a bad word to someone. It takes discipline and maturity to walk away.

I got my first taste of that at age seventeen, my first year of organized ball at Norfolk, Virginia. Some fans were giving me nasty comments, and I was real frustrated. After I slammed the bat in the dugout, my manager, Shaky Kain, took me off into a corner for a talk. He said, "Look, this is going to happen. More to you than others. And in language worse than you've been hearing. You gotta learn not to get mad. They're the characters who pay your salary. Let 'em holler all they want. Figure they're entitled. If you ever show them, or anyone, that they're getting to you, you're dead. Ignore. That's what you gotta do, ignore."

It was a hell of a speech, and I've always followed that advice.

27

THERE IS ALWAYS SOME KID WHO MAY BE SEEING ME FOR THE FIRST OR LAST TIME. I OWE HIM MY BEST

Joe DiMaggio was a great teammate and a perfect player. He did everything right on a ball field.
Archive Photos

I thought it might be appropriate to say a few words about Joe DiMaggio (who said the above) because of what he meant to the Yankees and to me. Truth is, I never saw a better all-around player. DiMag was a true professional. He had to be perfect every day, and he expected nothing less than the best from his teammates. We all had the feeling we were good, and Joe gave us that feeling. Seeing how much he wanted to win just gave you more confidence.

I was fortunate to be a teammate of DiMag's my first five years. Watching him, I learned a lot about leadership, what it meant to be a real pro. He played the game all out. He was quiet and distant, but he had incredible presence. I can still see him at his locker, by himself, legs crossed, smoking a cigarette, and the clubhouse man bringing him a cup of coffee. He rarely went out with us to dinner on the road. I think Eddie Lopat said he led the league in room service.

It was part of his mystique. DiMag never showed emotion; he made no excuses. People thought because of his coolness he was arrogant—he wasn't. He was a serious and proud man, proud of his ability, proud to be a Yankee. He expected to win, and he knew the team depended on him. He'd play hurt, and he expected you to do the same. If he saw something he didn't like, he'd give you that glare, or say it in a way you'd never forget.

In my second year with the Yankees, I sat out the second game of a doubleheader late in the year. I was tired. My backup, Gus Zerniel, didn't have a good game. That's when Joe wanted me to know that being a Yankee, being a professional, was deadly serious business. In the locker room afterward, Joe grumbled that a twenty-three-year-old kid should play both ends of a doubleheader, then he cursed. I got the message. The team needed me, just like the team needed him. I caught doubleheaders most of the rest of my career. Heck, I'd catch almost every game of the season. Casey always wanted me in there, even if I were fatigued or injured. But it was Joe who always left the big impression.

I remember my rookie year, when we stayed at the Hotel Edison. Joe would often buy my breakfast. He said that I didn't make the money he did, so this was his treat. You don't forget gestures like that. When I became a veteran player, I brought young guys like Bobby Richardson to dinner at our house in New Jersey. Joe helped make you feel that being a Yankee was special.

I admired DiMag. Funny, he came from a family of Italian immigrants and didn't finish school. Like me. He was really kind of shy, like me. He understood his value to the team and fought for every dollar at contract time. I did the same. He felt embarrassed when he struck out, which didn't happen much. I felt the same way. He had great respect for the way the game should be played. When I first came up, I was discouraged at times, and once sort of moped out to right field. Joe came over and said, "Never walk to your position, kid. It looks as if you aren't hustling."

A lot's been said and written about DiMag, especially about his personal life. It was sort of sad he was alone a lot, he wanted his privacy; he didn't have close family or friends. But I know what he meant to his teammates on the Yankees. Sure, he was kind of hard to get to know. But after he got to know you, he was a heck of a nice guy. We'd talk baseball for hours in the clubhouse or on the train; he always was encouraging to us. He had a tremendous hold on people.

When the Yankees honored me in 1959, DiMag was named the honorary chairman of Yogi Berra Day. That was a big thrill for me. Believe me, it's an honor to be linked with him. I wasn't comfortable batting cleanup when he retired—that was DiMag's spot.

For all his incredible individual skills and desire, DiMag was a great team man. Like I say, he was a perfect ballplayer, but he was all about winning. Nobody made you feel prouder to be a Yankee.

28

USUALLY WHEN YOU GET ONE OF THESE, YOU'RE DEAD OR GONE

In the Navy in 1944. I obeyed orders, kept my mouth shut, and did my duty. *Berra Archives*

I've been pretty fortunate my whole life. A lot of good things have happened to me, a lot of lucky things, too. I was real lucky not to get wounded or killed during the Normandy invasion.

When I was loading rockets into the breech and dropped one, our 36-foot rocket boat lurched and everyone dove under the gun mount. I thought it was the end and held my breath, but nothing else happened. I later got grazed on the hand by a bullet from a German machine-gun nest, but it wasn't serious.

Joe Garagiola always said nothing would ever happen to me—I was one of God's children.

My teammates always considered me a lucky guy. Once the Yankees were on a plane going through a bad storm. For some reason, I stayed back a few hours and took another plane. The players said they could see me reading the paper the next day with the headline "Yankee Team Killed in Plane Crash: Berra Lives—Catcher Takes Later Flight."

Truth is, I always considered myself lucky to be a major-league ballplayer, especially a Yankee, and fortunate to win three MVP awards, especially when others were deserving. And I always considered myself lucky to have a great wife and family and friends, and to have lived long enough to enjoy them.

It was Lou Gehrig who considered himself the luckiest man in the world. He died at only thirty-nine, but I understand what he meant in his farewell speech. He felt blessed to have a great family and friends and to be a Yankee. I never met Gehrig or saw him play, but his words always affected me. I always wanted to do something to honor his memory. When the Yankees held a special day for me when I was playing, we had all the proceeds sent for a scholarship at Columbia, Gehrig's alma mater.

Everything in my life, I owe to baseball. Like I said when I was inducted into the Hall of Fame in 1972, "It has given me more than I could ever hope for. I hope when I leave this game, I will put something back."

My hope is that today's players, as well off as they are, will also put something back. Especially in helping kids, giving them advice, giving them hope. There's no reason they shouldn't. They owe it to baseball—and to themselves.

Like I said, I've been extremely fortunate. I've received a lot of honors and awards; I've had days in my honor; a New York ferry boat named after me, as well as a college and minor-league stadium, and a museum, both at Montclair State University, near my home.

A couple of years ago, Rose Cali, a close friend of mine and Carm's, came up with the idea of the Yogi Berra Museum and Learning Center. She said it would be built by friends and be nonprofit. Instead of just being a place of memorabilia, it would be a place where school groups could learn about history, math, physics, and other subjects, all tied to baseball.

I was honored when Rose asked me. A museum and education center named for someone who just made it through the eighth grade. It's a beautiful place, and I'm real proud of it. A lot of people say it looks like Cooperstown. I'm there a lot and get a kick out of seeing the different ages, from kids to seniors, and all the school groups; even our volunteers go from young kids to older folks. That's the great thing about baseball—it connects all the generations.

We've had a lot of visitors from all over. I was especially touched when Ted Williams came up for our opening from Central Florida, where he lives and has his own museum. To me, there's no greater living legend than Ted; he fought in two wars, he's raised millions for cancer research, and he's the greatest hitter ever. We both serve on the Veterans Committee for the Hall of Fame and have become good friends through the years. He's had a couple of strokes and can't do much, but he's still as passionate about the game as ever. For him to come all the way up just for me was pretty special.

At the press conference, I was with Ted and some of my best friends in the game—Gil McDougald, Larry Doby,

Ralph Branca. In the audience were donors, family, and friends. It was an overwhelming experience, and I realized how glad I was to be there, too. When a reporter asked how it felt to have a museum named after me, I said it was great, "because usually when you get one of these, you're dead or gone."

29

ONLY IN AMERICA

My father, Pietro Berra *(left)*, and Giovanni Garagiola *(right)*, Joe's father, worked in the same brickyard and were real close. We lived at 5447 Elizabeth Avenue; the Garagiolas were across the street, at 5446 Elizabeth. *The Sporting News*

My pop was a tenant farmer in northern Italy, near Milan, before World War I. Those were pretty troubled days in Europe. He knew he'd never be able to raise a family there. He knew the right thing to do was to leave the Old Country with his friend, Giovanni Garagiola, for a new life in America.

They eventually found their way to St. Louis, where they both found jobs in the brick kilns. And they bought little wooden houses, almost identical, across the street from each other in a modest area populated by Italians. The place was like a Little Italy and was known as "Dago Hill." Now it's just "The Hill." Anyway, the Garagiolas lived at 5446 Elizabeth Avenue, we lived at 5447 Elizabeth.

As long as I can remember, my parents and the Garagiolas were closest friends. And my closest friend was always, and still is, Joe Garagiola. To this day, we always keep in touch, always call each other on our birthdays (I'm eight months older).

After working side by side in the brickyard, our fathers would play boccie in back of the Garagiolas' house. Our older brothers worked together as waiters. Joe and I grew up and shared our dreams together. As kids, we played ball in the streets and sandlots, went to school and St. Ambrose Church, fetched our fathers' beer, and later worked in Sears Roebuck together; we were inseparable. Joe and I were even the best man at each other's wedding (actually, we agreed on announcing our engagements on the same day, but I jumped the gun).

Around the age of twelve, Joe and I alternated pitching and catching for the Stags, our YMCA league baseball team. We both dreamed of becoming major-league players, despite our fathers thinking baseball was a waste of time. In the summer of 1941, when we were teenagers and got try-outs with the St. Louis Cardinals, Joe was offered a $500 bonus to sign; I wasn't. I wasn't jealous of Joe, just happy for him. That kind of money was unheard of for Joe's father, who used it for the final payment on his house. But I was discouraged because I thought I was just as good.

Because we were so close, we always supported each other. Always gave each other a boost. When Joe became a rookie with the Cardinals, I went to Sportsman's Park during the 1946 World Series to cheer and celebrate when the Cardinals won. Yet Joe kept singing my praises to reporters, even though I still was barely a major-leaguer. Joe was always taller, flashier, funnier than me. He also told a lot of stories about me, true or not true, I never minded; they were always funny.

Our lives and careers took dramatically different turns. Joe was a catcher with the Cardinals, Pirates, Cubs, and Giants, then got hurt and retired in 1954. I had the good fortune of playing twice as long with one team—the Yankees—and stayed in uniform a long time after that.

But few people impress me more than Joe. He has a saintlike passion to help others, which he does all the time. I can't help but admire what Joe's done in his life after baseball.

Nobody worked or studied harder to be a broadcaster, and Joe became a Hall of Famer. I still miss him doing *Game of the Week* and the *Today* show. But Joe has completely dedicated himself to helping the less fortunate. He's always raising money and providing supplies and health services to help Native American kids on the reservation in Arizona. He's become the public face of BAT (Baseball Assistance Team), which helps needy former players and their families who've fallen on hard times.

And Joe's become a one-man crusade to ban chewing tobacco. He was so upset by seeing friends get cancer and die from the stuff, he's taken it on himself to help get legislation passed and go around the country warning people about the dangers.

Maybe Joe wasn't a hero on the field, but he's sure one off it. We always laugh about the odds of two best friends, the sons of Italian immigrants growing up on Dago Hill in the 1930s, becoming major-leaguers. One million to one? Ten million to one?

I have to believe it's even greater than the odds of a Jewish man becoming the mayor of Dublin. When someone told me that, all I could say was, "Only in America."

30

I'D SEE IF I COULD FIND THE GUY THAT LOST IT, AND IF HE WAS POOR, I'D GIVE IT BACK

Whitey Ford was cool and cocky, and nobody was better in big games.
Archive Photos

That's what I once said when someone asked me about finding a million dollars. Only today, the poor guy who lost a million dollars would probably be a baseball owner. Only he wants you to think he's going to the poorhouse.

Like I always say, I don't begrudge the players for getting such huge salaries. I'd ask for the same thing if some owner was willing to pay. People always ask me: Will these contracts ever stop? Are you envious of the players? Will the disparity between teams ruin baseball? No, no, and no.

Everyone should stop bellyaching about the salaries. This is America. Everything is always overblown, especially entertainment. As long as there's a profit in baseball, owners will pay crazy salaries. They can't control themselves. When there's no profit, the salaries will come down.

Baseball has survived a lot of craziness, it will survive more foolish spending. I don't buy the theory that teams that don't spend don't win. I've seen too many teams spend a ton and not win. It's the owners' game. It's their money. If the so-called big-market owners don't care about the so-called small-market owners, who are we to worry about it?

Funny, I'm also always asked how baseball is related to business. You'd think I'd gotten an MBA in eighth grade or something. Truth is, baseball is a business. When I played, it was a game. Now it's an "industry." But to me, it's still baseball. And I love talking baseball, to anyone. I did with the alumni of the Harvard Business School a couple of years ago, and I talked baseball over breakfast with Milton Friedman, the economist. Baseball is always a good common denominator.

All I will say is that on good ball clubs and in good companies, you need team players to do the job, day in and day out. The Yankee teams I played on had a lot of platoon guys; versatile, interchangeable guys who performed wherever or whenever they played. Near the end of my career, I was even platooning with Elston Howard at catcher. This system would infuriate some guys, especially Gene Woodling or Hank Bauer when they'd be replaced, but Casey Stengel swore by this system. It kept everyone sharp and alert. Even the most marginal guy knew he'd get his chance to shine.

I think the same is true with businesses. You need the regular employees, the factory worker, computer programmer, or middle manager, to perform and feel important. You always hear that companies don't want any heroes, just grunts. Maybe because the CEO is always the hero. I think the big difference between baseball and business is that a lot of companies aren't good at crediting or rewarding their valuable people. And that can hurt morale.

Obviously, the CEO can't watch his or her hundreds or thousands of employees the way a manager does his players. But baseball really values its unsung heroes, like a Bucky Dent or a Luis Sojo. Without them, teams don't win. Companies should value their unsung people, too. Without them, they don't succeed. They should share the credit. That's the great thing about baseball. When you win, there's a oneness. You're a team, everyone's the same, everyone shares in the rewards. And it makes you hungrier to win again.

A last word about business and baseball. I was probably one of the first ballplayers to have an agent. His name was Frank Scott, and he used to be our traveling secretary with the Yankees, until he quit in 1950. One day he was at my house and saw a stack of wristwatches. When I told him that's what I usually received for a speech or appearance, Scott offered to represent me. He said I should be doing better than getting a wristwatch. Frank never negotiated my contracts—I always did—but he helped me earn some money in the off-season setting up appearances on shows like *Phil Silvers* and *Ed Sullivan,* and even some endorsements.

One of the things Frank arranged for me was a TV commercial for cat food in 1960 with me playing me and Whitey Ford being the voice of a cat. I remember my teammates were joshing me pretty good afterward. So I asked what was so funny. How many of them ever got nicely paid, talking to a cat?

31

I'D RATHER BE THE
YANKEE CATCHER THAN
THE PRESIDENT

The Stags, our old gang from The Hill, came to
Yankee Stadium to visit with me and Joe Garagiola.
Berra Archives

Being a professional athlete, I never considered myself special—just fortunate. I happened to do something I loved. It was a great life, something I wouldn't have traded for anything.

Sometimes it's hard to appreciate the impact baseball and other sports have on people. You play them as a kid, then you're hooked for life. People come up to me all the time and recall exact details of ball games they went to years ago. Baseball is full of memories, it's a big part of American life. Maybe that's why even presidents feel so attached to it.

Actually, I couldn't believe how much the game meant to some of the presidents I got to meet. Dwight Eisenhower was a huge ball fan. He attended a number of our World Series and wrote a congratulations letter to Don Larsen after his perfect game. Eisenhower told me when he grew up in Kansas, his real dream was to become a major-leaguer.

Funny how things work out. In World War II, Eisenhower was a general and I was a nineteen-year-old second-class Navy seaman. Thousands of us were in the English Channel, awaiting the word to move in on Omaha Beach, off the coast of France. But the weather was terrible and Eisenhower put the D-Day invasion back a day. We were anxious; putting it off a day only added to the tension.

Before dawn on June 6, 1944, Eisenhower ordered "Operation Overlord," the code name for the attack. Our crew of six unloaded from the USS *Bayfield* to our little rocket boat, moving past hundreds of other ships. Then Eisenhower came over the loudspeaker. He gave us a pep talk about the invasion, said that it was a great moment in history, that every man had to do his part to make it a success.

For me, there wasn't time to be scared. I said my prayers, then we worked like the devil to load the guns, shoot them, and keep our boat moving. We must have been out there six hours until the beachhead was finally secured.

I never did talk military stuff with Eisenhower when he became president. Or John Kennedy, who was a Navy man like me. JFK kidded me once that he was a real big Red Sox fan and kept close tabs on them, not the Yankees. You could tell sports was still important to these guys.

Probably the biggest presidential baseball fan was Nixon. He loved the game. I think he said if he had to do it all over again, he'd be a sportswriter. I think he also understood what I meant by "it ain't over 'til it's over," because he said, "I never leave a game before the last pitch, because in baseball, as in life and politics, you never know what will happen."

I golfed with Gerald Ford and practiced once with George Bush, who were both good athletes in their day. Ford's a real nice fellow, real calm. I remember Joe Garagiola, who was with him when he lost in 1976, said, "I'd seen Enos Slaughter get more upset about an umpire saying 'strike two' than Gerald Ford did when he realized he wasn't going to win the presidential election."

Being a president is the hardest job in the world. So I think sports—talking or watching it—is enjoyable to them. It's a welcome break from everything. When I was with the Yankees, we never had a Rose Garden ceremony like they do today. But you could see that Reagan and Clinton really enjoyed those events. Just look at pictures of presidents throwing out the first ball of the season, they're really enjoying themselves. They're two great American traditions—baseball and the presidency.

Being around Harry Truman in 1947 when he threw out the first ball in Griffith Stadium in Washington made me real nervous. It was the first game of my rookie year, but my hands were shaking because this was the *president*. It was one of the few times I was in awe of somebody.

People tell me that presidents and other politicians sometimes quote me during their speeches. I guess it's kind of flattering. Though it was kind of interesting to hear my name come up a lot during Clinton's impeachment hearings. One of the president's lawyers was getting frustrated and said, "We've gone well beyond Yogi Berra land. It's déjà vu all over again and again."

I guess baseball and politics always sort of mixed. George

W. Bush owned the Texas Rangers, now he's running the country. People laugh at his malapropisms; I just hope I'm not the cause. He admitted carrying the book of my quotes with him while campaigning in New Hampshire, then told reporters that he'd like to have Yogi Berra in his administration. He said I'd be a good press spokesman because I could always say, "I really didn't say everything I said."

That's not bad. But my advice to any politician is what I used to tell the press when I was managing the Yankees: "If you ask me a question I don't know, I'm not going to answer."

32

MOST PEOPLE KNOW ME
BY MY FACE

Reading to my son Larry, who's now a Civil War expert and a voracious reader. *The Sporting News*

Being a well-known person doesn't mean people really know you. People always expect me to be funny. I guess that's the popular image. "Make up a Yogi-ism," they'll say. I can't. I don't think I ever said anything intentionally funny in my life. Sometimes the quotes just happen—I just don't know when I'll say them.

Once a couple visiting our museum met me and asked if I could say a Yogi-ism. I told them I don't make them up on the spot. I said if I could, I'd be famous. I consider myself serious but don't take myself too seriously. Sometimes people tell me I look like Yogi Berra, and I say, "Yeah, a lot of people tell me that."

Truth is, I consider myself shy. I do meet many people, but I don't say much—I usually let them do the talking. You can learn a lot by paying attention to what someone says and how they say it. Sometimes you can tell if a person's sincere and interesting or phony and just wasting your time. Whatever, I always try to be respectful.

I will say it's uncomfortable, even embarrassing, when people make a big deal about meeting me. My son Dale likes telling about the time I was signing autographs at a school fund-raiser. A very excited fellow in his fifties came up to me and said, "Yogi Berra! My God! This is like witnessing the Second Coming!" I just looked at him and said, "That good, huh?"

I think the relationship between fans and athletes has changed through the years. There are a lot more demands on athletes now, especially with the money they make. Fans and glad-handers and the media expect them to give more of themselves, especially their time. That isn't always easy, especially in the off-season. Players have families; they're entitled to privacy, too.

There are lots of professional athletes who are great guys. They get behind charities, they help kids, they sign autographs, they're kind and gentle. Unfortunately, the ones who get in trouble off the field create the bad image.

I always considered playing professional sports an honor. Especially with the Yankees. A certain conduct was expected of you. You never wanted to embarrass the organization. Tommy Henrich, who was a great teammate and leader when I was a rookie in 1947, once said, "I hope the pride a player has in being a Yankee doesn't die out. It's more than a tradition. It's a mental, almost physical, lift for a player to put on a Yankee uniform. . . . The spirit which was born here with Babe Ruth should never die."

I hope he's right. I've always tried to carry out that responsibility in public, too. I've always tried to be cooperative with the media, sign fan autographs, act in a respectable way. I'm no more special than anybody else. I just try to treat everyone the same, whether it's the guy pumping gas or the vice president of a bank.

I was happy to be a ballplayer. Now I'm happy to be retired and enjoying my family. I still do a lot of public events, but I really do love being home. Wherever my grandkids go, people always ask them, "What's it like to have Yogi Berra as your grandfather?" And they always say, "Why? He's just Grandpa." That makes me feel pretty good.

33

I LOVE MOVIES
WHEN I LIKE THEM

As a manager in 1964, I did a little pitching in during
batting practice. *Berra Archives*

Don't ask me why, but I've always been a movie nut. It started as a kid, when we'd see three pictures for a nickel on Sundays. Who knew years later I'd get paid to review them?

In those days, there was no TV. We didn't go on vacations. Our world was The Hill, a small neighborhood with neat framed houses and religious shrines in the yards. So movies captured our imaginations—it was fun to watch stuff like *Tarzan*. Who knew what Africa looked like except seeing it in the movies?

If not for the movies, I'd never have gotten the name Yogi. My friends saw a travelogue about India, and one of the people in it was a Hindu fakir, a yogi, who was meditating. Because I used to sit with my arms folded and legs crossed, my buddies said I looked like the yogi in the movie.

I loved westerns, adventures, dramas, comedies, you name

it. I was a big Greer Garson fan and really loved the Marx Brothers; when I was twenty-one and playing for Newark, I saw *A Night in Casablanca* in all eight cities of the International League.

When I joined the Yankees, my teammates always asked my opinion of a movie, because they knew I'd likely seen it. I remember DiMaggio always trusted my opinions. Anyway, I usually saw movies as a fun way to kill a couple of hours.

Once on a road trip I saw *The Pink Panther,* and I loved it so much I immediately took Carm and the kids to see it when I got home. I think I embarrassed them because I was laughing so loud.

I'm a little tough on baseball films because a lot of them don't smack too real. If I had to pick the best, I'd say *Eight Men Out,* about the 1919 Black Sox scandal. It was a good morality story; you could really see how the players were exploited, how they were tempted, how they struggled with their conscience. The actors did a great job with the baseball stuff, too.

I have a pretty good appreciation for actors, having done some commercials and a couple of cameos. Mickey Mantle, Roger Maris, and I appeared in *A Touch of Mink* with Doris Day and Cary Grant—that was fun. And I once was a brain surgeon—no kidding—in a *General Hospital* episode, in the early '60s. Those were the days before the soaps got sexy.

Becoming a film critic on TV in the late 1980s was great because I got to see a lot of interesting movies. I remember the first one was *Fatal Attraction,* of which I said I was scared only during the scary parts and referred to Glenn Close as Glen Cove, but I can't really remember if I gave it a single, double, triple, or home run.

Truth is, I don't have any real pearls of wisdom about movies. I still watch a lot of old movies on TV, sometimes forgetting I've seen them already. Some you don't forget. *Saving Private Ryan,* that was pretty strong, all too realistic for any veteran. Some are just a waste of time. What else can I say except movies are a matter of personal taste. It's really hard to take any critic's reviews to heart—especially a movie nut like me.

34

IN BASEBALL, YOU DON'T KNOW NOTHING

Signing my last contract as a player in 1963, with manager Ralph Houk *(left)* and owner Dan Topping *(center)*. *Ernie Sisto/The New York Times*

Baseball is a lot like life because you never know. Things happen that don't make a lot of sense. Being fired as manager by the Yankees in my first year after going to the World Series sure didn't make sense to me. Or being told by Branch Rickey, the greatest talent evaluator in baseball, that I'd never be a major-league player.

Later on, maybe that did make sense. Rickey, who was running the Cardinals at the time of my tryout, knew he'd be leaving to go to Brooklyn and maybe was trying to hide me. Because the next year, he sent me a telegram to report to the Dodgers' training camp in Bear Mountain, but by then I had signed with the Yankees.

Still, rejections are a big part of life. Like job interviews. You can say and do all the right things, but you never really know. My biggest rejections were as manager. I was hired three times, fired three times, even though I had a winning record in each job. The only thing I know is, that's baseball.

The big thing is to make decisions and issue orders and stand by them. Above all, be yourself. When managers try to act like someone they're not, they lose respect. When people asked me in 1964 if I would manage like Casey Stengel or Ralph Houk, I said, "I'll manage like Yogi Berra."

I admit when the Yankees fired me as manager that season, I was stunned. It was my first year as manager. We had a lot of injuries but pulled together and almost won the World Series. When I got called into owner Dan Topping's office the day after the Series, I thought I was getting a contract extension. I got fired instead. Why? Supposedly because I wasn't in control of the players. I think the harmonica incident was the big thing. That's when Phil Linz played a harmonica on a team bus in August after a tough loss. I told him to knock it off. When he didn't hear me, I kind of swatted it away. The papers made a big to-do about it. But from that point on, we started to get hot and moved into first place. I honestly thought the guys played hard for me. I just didn't have the support of the general manager, Ralph Houk. While the Yankees offered me another job after the firing, I thought it best to go somewhere else. I didn't bad-mouth anybody. I thanked the Yankees for the opportunity. Like that rule says, "It's not what happens to you, but how you handle it that matters."

That's when I joined Casey Stengel, my old manager, as a coach with the Mets. Leaving a situation where I'd put in a lot of years and made great friends was difficult. But that's baseball—that's life. Besides, Casey was always loyal to me when I was a player, and I never forgot that. He wanted me on his staff and to work with the young guys. I didn't get mad at the Yankees or wish them any ill feelings. I simply got a chance to stay in New York, and I spent ten great years with the Mets. I was a coach on the 1969 championship team and managed them into the World Series in '73.

When I got fired in 1975, it was sort of a similar thing. I didn't have the support of the owner, M. Donald Grant, because I wanted to discipline one of our players, Cleon Jones, who was insubordinate. When Grant wouldn't let me, it hurt my authority. When you don't have the backing of your boss, you've got nothing. I didn't think it was right I was fired. But things did work out. I rejoined the Yankees as a coach in 1976, and we were becoming a championship team again.

What did I learn? A baseball manager is like a CEO. To get results, you treat people the way you'd want to be treated. If I had a problem with a player, I'd talk it over with him in private—I'd never embarrass him. Being a manager is a high-pressure situation, there's a load of responsibility, plus there's not a lot of job security. So control what you can control. In any big job, you're always second-guessed and probably get blamed more than you should.

If you do get fired, so be it. Don't obsess over it. Any time you take an important job like being a manager, you know you can always get fired. When you do, just let go of it. It's time to move forward, move toward something new and different.

People ask if I felt any satisfaction when the Yankees

and Mets went bad after I got fired as manager. Honestly, no. I still felt attachments to the players. I had a lot of friends in both places. Besides, in my heart, I felt I was doing a pretty good job. Sometimes in baseball, you don't know nothing.

35

WE HAVE DEEP DEPTH

Playing baseball was all I ever wanted to do.
If I had to do it over again, I'd do it again.
Archive Photos

Why do some teams pull together and perform at the highest level? What makes team chemistry?

Businesspeople often ask me those questions, and I just tell them about some of the Yankee teams I played on. We had dedicated guys who had great pride. Not rah-rah guys, but solid veterans who always kept you on your toes, even on the little things. I remember Tommy Henrich telling young guys like Jerry Coleman to call for pop-ups because, "This is the Yankees. We're a family. We don't have any secrets among us. If you want the ball, *yell* for it."

We policed ourselves—heck, we never even let Casey Stengel, our manager, in our meetings.

You did feel like a family being part of the Yankees, like we were brothers. No question it helped that we traveled everywhere by train, where we ate together, played cards together, went over the papers, and talked baseball. We really were a true team and were confident we'd win—that was the Yankee culture we grew up in. Winning was always the bottom line.

Nowadays most teams have captains, and I'm not going to knock that. Leadership is important. But in all the years I was with the Yankees, from when I came up in 1946 and finished in 1963, we never had a captain, and I don't think our leadership suffered one bit.

When I became a manager in 1964, people said I should appoint a captain. What for? I believed everyone should have the same rank. They're all in the same boat. Make everybody the same and who's going to gripe? In all my years with the Yankees, nobody ever got into a fight with another teammate.

A real good example of the specialness of a team was the 1949 Yankees. That was the first year of our dynasty. We had a new manager, Casey, and a mixture of veterans, rookies, and young guys like myself. We had aging stars like Joe DiMaggio and Tommy Henrich, and a bunch of platoon players.

We also had some doubts, coming off a disappointing season in 1948. There was worry that DiMag might miss the season because of his injured foot. Plus we looked bad in exhibition games. Right before the season, Charley Keller, who was a strong home run hitter before he hurt his back, called a meeting. Told us it was time to get serious. Told us we were a team. He warned us that other clubs were beginning to think we were a one-man team, meaning DiMaggio, meaning that we better not use Joe's absence as an excuse.

All season long, we had a lot of injuries, me included with a broken thumb. But I think Charley's talk kind of stirred us, because all the guys kept picking each other up. We were a patchwork team, but everyone contributed. When I was hurt, my backup, Charlie Silvera, came in and did a superb job. Charlie scarcely played after that season with the Yankees. I'd catch almost every game of the season, including doubleheaders. Charlie was a good-natured guy, a great teammate, and never complained. He warmed up guys in the bullpen, he'd break in a new glove for me and lug equipment and still not complain. He was just glad to be a Yankee and help in any way he could.

During one off-season, Charlie was speaking to some inmates in a New Jersey prison. "You probably never heard of me," he said. "And I probably should think about introducing myself to Casey Stengel, too."

In one particular season, Charlie only got to bat nine times. Every year, the Yankees would bring lots of catchers into camp, but you could see why they always kept Charlie. He was a role player who always put the team first. Whenever called on, he played well. He was good for our team chemistry. Any successful organization and team needs depth, and we had guys like Charlie Silvera—guys you could count on.

36

IF THE WORLD WERE
PERFECT, IT WOULDN'T BE

Even before I was known as "Yogi," I used to fold
my arms. That's my little sister Josie in the front.
Berra Archives

Everyone has flaws and makes mistakes—nobody's perfect. I'm no social philosopher, but if there's anything I've learned in baseball and life, it's the importance of treating people with respect and being tolerant.

Baseball is like society—it's governed by rules and decisions and you have to respect them. Even imperfect ones. You even have to learn to accept bad calls by umpires; although nowadays it seems they get less respect and more abuse.

I don't want to sound soft on umpires, because I never was. But too many players blame their failings on umpires, there's too many Alibi Ikes. Umpires are human. They miss calls. Life goes on. That's not to say I didn't give them a piece of my mind a few times. About the maddest I ever got was when Jackie Robinson stole home in the 1955 World Series—he was out and still is out—but Bill Summers called him safe and I wasn't, let's say, too tolerant of his call.

But I learned something basic about having someone leaning over my back and helping determine the outcome of a game: Don't antagonize him. Don't show him up. Don't dwell on his mistakes. Argue if you must, but move on. It's the same in life. Nobody likes a hothead. People who disagree or argue all the time come off as self-righteous, plus you lose credibility. If I had a beef with an umpire because I *knew* he was wrong, I let him know it but wouldn't lose my mind over it. I played in over 2,000 major-league games and got thrown out only three or four times—not bad considering all the disagreements I've had with umps.

Honesty and consistency, that's all you ask for in umps. I'd try to get to know them, too. One in particular, Nestor Chylak, developed a trust in me—he'd sometimes ask, "Did I get that one right?" after making a close call. When umpires missed a pitch, I would say, "You missed that one," or "You're a better ump than that." But I'd never turn around and tell them because that would show them up— and umps *hate* being shown up. I think umps took more guff from me than they did most catchers before kicking them out. I think they knew I wasn't trying to embarrass them. And I never—well, hardly never—used profane language.

Like all authority figures, umps have different temperaments. By the end of my career, I knew how far you could push these guys. I learned that an ump named Cal Hubbard wasn't a guy you could debate with. One night in Cleveland, I thought Hubbard missed a couple of calls, and when I beefed about one, I stepped in front of the plate and threw the ball back hard to Tommy Byrne, our pitcher. I didn't realize that Hubbard, who was a huge former football player, was coming right after me. As I turned, Hubbard was right in my face, hollering like crazy. When I told him I didn't have to take this, he shot back, "One more word out of you, Berra, your ass is out of here." Call me stubborn, but I had to add, "Say you missed it, and I'll shut up." Call him stubborn, too, because he immediately ejected me.

Like I said, I generally got along good with umpires. You're inches away from the guy for over two hours, how could you not? Vic Wertz used to call me the last of the playing umpires, but I think umps kind of warmed up to me. Even Hubbard, who later had some fun with me. I remember he'd warn a hitter on a 3-2 pitch that he'd better be ready to swing because he, Hubbard, "is liable to miss it." That can get into a hitter's head, and that's good for us. I'll never forget one year during a brutally hot day in Boston, I was dead tired and desperately trying to get thrown out of the game. So I started insulting Hubbard, the plate ump, hoping that would do it. But he wouldn't budge. "Berra, if I'm gonna be out here in this heat," he said, "you're gonna stay right here with me."

Few people know this, but it was actually an umpire, Bill McGowan, who first popularized my name in the major leagues. Real early in my career, McGowan arranged for me to autograph a couple of baseballs. He looked at the balls and said, "Who the hell put this Larry Berra on here?" When I told him I did because that's my name, he said, "The hell it is. Sign them Yogi. That's your name, ain't it?" I didn't bother to argue.

THE FUTURE AIN'T WHAT
IT USED TO BE

The groundbreaking for our museum and learning
center in 1998 was a good cause to celebrate.
Chang Lee/The New York Times

Times change, life is short. How many times do you hear that stuff? It's true. Everything's faster paced nowadays—two-career families, fancy technology, everyone's always in a rush, rush, rush. The big thing is priorities. The business world, even the baseball world, may change a lot, but that doesn't mean you should ever compromise your values. Like I've said, I'd be pretty dumb if suddenly I started being something I'm not.

Baseball was a good career; it provided a good life. We never got great salaries—remember, this was well before agents and free agency, so almost all ballplayers worked in the off-season as salesmen and at other jobs. We had families to support. But I took advantage of opportunities, and that helped me prepare for my family's financial security.

I was fortunate in baseball to make lasting friendships. One of my closest buddies, Phil Rizzuto (who is my oldest son Larry's godfather), and I invested in the bowling business in the '50s before the boom and sold it before the crash. Doing appearances and endorsements helped. So did getting my teammates to promote Yoo-Hoo. That's the chocolate drink company that I did some PR for and wound up having an active interest in as a vice president in the '60s. Bottom line is, I'd never let what happened off the field affect me on the field. I learned that from Casey Stengel, who was pretty well-to-do but would never talk business.

One of the beneficial things in baseball is its emphasis on rituals and organization—things like spring training, batting practice, workouts, team meetings. There's a structure to everything. You need a strong commitment to play baseball; it requires practice and discipline. No question, some of those rituals still keep my life in balance. I'm still very committed to regularly working out, keeping my Wednesday night card games, going to church, playing a lot of golf, watching what I eat, and watching baseball. Really, though, the constant is staying active—I've done it my whole life.

Like most things, baseball is a people business. You have to listen. Be flexible and personal. Find out how to get the best out of people. That's what I mean when I say you observe a lot by watching. We all got along real good on the Yankees. But as a catcher, I needed the trust of my pitchers for us to succeed. You treat each guy different because each *is* different. If Whitey Ford was struggling, I'd get him a little mad, and I knew the batter would be in trouble. Say with Bob Turley, you'd have to pet him a little, give him more encouragement. Not everyone's the same. We always say those Yankee teams were like a family. And all families have a different makeup.

Speaking of family, my main concern today is our family, our nine grandchildren, and their well-being. Honestly, I don't think much about the future—not like I used to—but just enjoy life. It's too short to worry about.

38

ALWAYS GO TO OTHER PEOPLE'S FUNERALS, OTHERWISE THEY WON'T GO TO YOURS

With Mom and our first baby, Larry Jr. We were still living with my parents at the time. *Berra Archives*

Let's just say I'm a real loyal person. Loyalty affects you on a daily basis—with family, with friends, and in your profession. It's a matter of trust and respect. It's not an automatic thing. It's not an I'll-do-this-for-you-if-you-do-this-for-me deal. Loyalty is a selfless proposition.

If people trust you, and you're careful not to violate that trust, there's nothing you can't accomplish. Without my brothers' loyalty, I never would've gotten a chance to pursue baseball. Without the Yankees' loyalty, I never would've been able to play my whole career in one city and enjoy a good life. Without the loyalty of my family and friends, I'd never be able to share so many good moments in their lives.

Loyalty, though, seems to be fading these days. At least it's missing a lot in professional sports and in business. Good workers who didn't screw up used to be almost guaranteed lifetime jobs in one company—that inspired loyalty. Now that's almost unheard of. Management gives employees little

164

stake in the business, and many workers feel as disposable as yesterday's newspaper.

When I played ball, there was no free agency. And even though I had some contract disputes, I always felt a strong emotional connection—loyalty—to my team. I know the Yankees were very loyal to me, because I played seventeen years there. They even gave me a chance to manage; a job they wouldn't even trust Babe Ruth with.

But the money in the game has changed everything. Players feel little loyalty to their team—and owners feel little loyalty to the players. The players are interchangeable, and rosters are like revolving doors. Money overwhelms loyalty, and that's unfortunate.

How to get more loyalty in baseball and business? Maybe more personal involvement. Why not give workers a real stake in their company, offer them stock ownership? The same with baseball. With the salaries so exorbitant, why not give the players part ownership? Maybe you'll see more attachment, more loyalty.

I've seen how an owner's personal connection to players affects loyalty. John McMullen, who lives in my town and used to own the Houston Astros and New Jersey Devils, is a real good friend. When I was fired as Yankee manager in 1985, he brought me down to Houston the next year to be a coach. I found him always honest and caring; he was a real father figure to the players. He got criticized for trying to hold the line on salaries, but he got to know his players and did an awful lot for them and their families. And they were pretty loyal to John in return.

Same with the Devils. I know a lot of their players could've gotten more money with other teams, but they remained in New Jersey because of their loyalty to John. In 1999–2000, his last season as owner, they dedicated winning the Stanley Cup to him. That's because he treated them like he'd treat his sons; he had their utmost respect.

John was an old-fashioned owner. To him, loyalty in sports was becoming old-fashioned, too. There was one thing I always insisted to him in Houston. I'd be a coach, but never his manager. As our wives were also close friends, I never wanted to do anything to affect our friendships. I was too loyal to him for that.

39

NINETY PERCENT OF SHORT PUTTS DON'T GO IN

Another shot I wish I had over again.
Berra Archives

Next to baseball, golf is my favorite passion. It's a great way to relax and get exercise—when it isn't frustrating as hell. Seriously, golf is a great outlet, a nice way to forget about the little things that are bothering you. Fresh air. Green grass. Some laughs. Friendly competition. And for an older guy like me, who's always been competitive, golf allows me to still compete. I'm not that good—I have a real ugly swing and have always said I could hit a baseball farther than I ever could a golf ball. But I still love to beat my friends; it gives me a kick.

Golf's real popular these days. It's a big social thing and that's great. But I've been playing for about fifty years and I enjoy the purity of it, I really do. I play golf with my sons, and we have a lot of fun, though I liked it better when I could beat them. And I've been real lucky to meet and play with a lot of interesting people—former presidents, like

Gerald Ford and George Bush, basketball guys like Michael Jordan and Julius Erving, and a lot of pro women golfers—even the great Babe Didrikson Zaharias, who I had a lot of fun with. She and her husband, George, who was a wrestler, owned a course in St. Petersburg where the Yankees trained.

It's a great game and a humbling game. But you also get to strategize and learn something about yourself. I learned to shoot righty (although I still putt lefty) back in the '50s when I was having a terrible round. On one hole, I borrowed my partner's right-handed clubs and hit my best shot of the day. I finished with a good round and have played right-handed ever since. I've also had a whole lot of not-so-good days. I remember complaining once that I knew my shot would land in the water. When my friend Kevin Carroll said, "Come on, Yogi, think positively," I said, "OK, I'm positive my shot is going into the water."

One of the things I appreciate about golf is that it can be very useful. Celebrity golf tournaments raise millions of dollars to help kids and worthwhile charities, and I play in as many as I can. I'm real proud of my own tournament at the Montclair Country Club, which in nine years has raised over $1 million to help special needs scouts. Whenever I see the smiles on these kids' faces at our tournament I know all the preparation and hard work is worth it.

Besides baseball, I've always been involved in leisure sports. I've always felt there is a great deal to be gained in playing them—I saw it firsthand when we owned a bowling alley and a racquetball club. It's a great release. It's fun. It's exercise. It's a good way to get away from stress. Everybody should have a release, something to clear the mind and a way to find a little enjoyment and peace. For Ted Williams, it was always fishing. For Carmen, it's her morning walks. For me, it's always a round of golf.

40

IT'S OVER

Carm and I return to Yankee Stadium in 1999—it was
a long time coming. *Berra Archives*

I've always been a devout Catholic. The St. Ambrose Church was a major part of our life on The Hill. I'd catch heck from Pop if I ever missed confession on Saturday afternoon, and our whole neighborhood went to church every Sunday morning. To this day, I regularly attend five o'clock mass and go to church every Sunday.

I've always believed in brotherhood, redemption, and forgiveness. But my firing by George Steinbrenner as Yankee manager in 1985 was more than hurtful and disappointing. It struck deeper than that.

The hurt wasn't so much that I was fired. Or that it was only sixteen games into the season. Or that George had promised that I'd be the manager all season, no matter what. Heck, nobody knows better than me that managers are hired to get fired. What bothered me most was the disrespect; to me, that was unforgivable.

George didn't tell me face-to-face that I was fired. He

had somebody else do it. That was real tough to accept. I felt I deserved better. Especially after all I had given to the Yankees in thirty years as a player, coach, and manager.

Like I said, I'd been fired before, but I was always told in person by the owner. I wasn't happy about this firing, but I never lashed out at anybody, including George. "What's the use of getting angry?" I told the reporters. "I did the best I could, and the players did, too."

At some point, I decided not to go back to Yankee Stadium as long as George was in charge. I always knew working under George was tough. I knew he was impulsive and hands-on. I'd seen his battles with Billy Martin (I was a coach then); I'd seen his tirades. And I always knew he'd be meddling with me as manager. I'm patient, George is anything but. When someone asked about our relationship, I said, "We agree different."

That may have been an understatement. In 1984, my first year managing under him, he was blaming me for something in my office and I lost my cool and threw a pack of cigarettes at him. George triggered an anger I didn't know I had.

For fourteen years, I stayed away from Yankee Stadium. It was a matter of principle and pride. And stubbornness. The Yankees tried everything to entice me back. They put up a plaque in my honor, but I stayed away. Old-Timers games, I stayed away. My closest friends, guys like Phil Rizzuto and Whitey Ford, pleaded with me to come back. Even the managers who succeeded me, from Lou Piniella to Joe Torre, kept trying to get me. Many people kept telling me to forget George, I was a Yankee, I belonged there. But I had made a very personal decision, and I wasn't budging.

In December 1998, two months after the Yankees' record-breaking season and World Series win, I was approached again. Suzyn Waldman, a broadcaster for the Yankees who was close to George, asked him if he would be willing to fly from Tampa to visit me at our museum and privately apologize so we could finally bury the hatchet. George was agreeable, only if I was agreeable to seeing him. My immediate instinct was to say no. It seemed like just another scheme to break me down and make me return to Yankee Stadium. I was upset about it, until my son Dale spoke to me. He said that if George was man enough to come see me, which wouldn't be easy for him, I should do the honorable thing and meet him. Then Dale mentioned that out of respect, my grandchildren had never been to Yankee Stadium. It would be nice for them to go with me one day.

Maybe I've mellowed. I agreed to see George, who I think has also mellowed. The only thing I insisted was that Carmen be included in the meeting. On January 5, 1999, George and I and Carmen had a heartfelt talk for fifteen minutes. George apologized and said all the right things. He said that how he fired me was the worst mistake he'd made in baseball. I told him I made a lot of mistakes in baseball, too. I said, "Fourteen years is long enough. It's over."

Then I gave George a tour of the museum. I think he appreciated what a tribute it was to Yankee history. Later, we went on Suzyn's radio show, and he talked of how with

DiMaggio ailing, and with the Yankees being champs again, he felt a big need in making me part of the Yankees again.

Things have been terrific with me and George since (though I admit it's nice I don't work for him anymore). I've been back to Yankee Stadium numerous times and feel real welcome there. The Yankees even had a special day for me—the first time my grandchildren saw the Stadium—and David Cone made it extra special by pitching a perfect game.

As I told my family, fourteen years wasn't bad for a grudge—I guess I made my point. Now there is forgiveness and conciliation. I really have no regrets.